Economic Principles in Action

Robert L. Moore

Unemployment

Money

Exchange Rates

Efficiency

Competition

Pricing

Inflation

Elasticity

Demand

Stagflation

Supply

Labor

Equity

ECONOMIC
PRINCIPLES
IN ACTION

ROBERT L. MOORE *Occidental College, Los Angeles*

ECONOMIC PRINCIPLES IN ACTION

Prentice-Hall, Inc., Englewood Cliffs, N.J. 07632

Library of Congress Cataloging in Publication Data

    Main entry under title:

    Economic principles in action.

        Includes index.
        1. Economics--Addresses, essays, lectures.
    I. Moore, Robert L., (date)
    HB34.E236   330   79-4327
    ISBN 0-13-226845-0

Cover design by Edsal Enterprises
Manufacturing buyer: Ed Leone

Printed in the United States of America

10 9 8 7 6 5 4 3 2 1

Prentice-Hall International, Inc., *London*
Prentice-Hall of Australia Pty. Limited, *Sydney*
Prentice-Hall of Canada, Ltd., *Toronto*
Prentice-Hall of India Private Limited, *New Delhi*
Prentice-Hall of Japan, Inc., *Tokyo*
Prentice-Hall of Southeast Asia Pte. Ltd., *Singapore*
Whitehall Books Limited, *Wellington, New Zealand*

PH 12-6-79

ACKNOWLEDGMENTS

My debt to others in putting together this book is enormous. In some sense, the work was actually a joint effort of the Economics 10 Staff at Harvard University over the past several years. Several times I was not the person to "discover" a particular article. Often times, other people were invloved in the development of the questions (and answers) that accompany each article. In addition, introductory economics students at both Harvard University and Occidental College have greatly improved the quality of the questions and answers. I cannot begin to name all of these people. However, I would like to especially thank Bob William, Jeff Wolcowitz, Dani Kaufman, Elisabeth Allison, Ken Froewiss, George Feiger, Amy Taylor, Steve Allen, Harvey Rosen, Lee Hansen, and Susan May for specific help in finding various articles or writing questions to accompany them. I still cannot recall how several of the articles first came to my attention and I regret any omissions in this regard. Rosemary Johnson and Susanne McCarthy helped enormously in various administrative matters relating to this book. Thanks are also due all the talented people at Prentice-Hall who helped in this project. Finally, David Hemenway and Otto Eckstein deserve my special thanks for encouraging me to undertake this project. Unfortunately I must accept full responsibility for any errors or defects.

Robert L. Moore
Occidental College

CONTENTS*

*For convenience, the titles of some articles have been condensed.

Ando, Albert
Bach, G. Leland
Burks, Edward C.
Clark, Lindley H., Jr.
Cook, William J.
Dale, Edwin L., Jr.
Foldessy, Edward P.
Freeman, Richard
Friedman, Milton

Garino, David P.
Geczi, Michael L.
Gordon, R.A.
Heilbroner, Robert L.
Heller, Walter, W.
Hilder, David B.
Hollomon, J. Herbert
Ingrassia, Paul
Kilborn, Peter T.

Klein, Lawrence
Kwitny, Jonathon
Lenzner, Robert
Loeb, Marshall
Miller, Gay Sands
Modigliani, Franco
Nicholson, Tom
Okun, Arthur M.

Pearlstine, Norman
Prial, Frank J.
Samuelson, Paul
Savoy, Maggie
Sterba, James P.
Tobin, James
Williams, John D.
Wilson, David B.

OBJECTIVES AND KEY CONCEPTS*

I. *THE BASIC TOOLS—SUPPLY, DEMAND, AND ELASTICITY IN ACTION*

"Moonshiners in South Find Sales Are Down as Their Costs Go Up"

Objectives: To translate various statements into appropriate supply and demand curves; to use the concept of elasticity of demand to determine how total revenue changes in response to price change.

Key Concepts: demand curve, supply curve, factor market vs. product market, substitute goods, complementary goods, price elasticity of demand.

"Wine Talk"

Objectives: To evaluate various statements about the workings of supply and demand; to clarify the meaning of "economic shortage."

Key Concepts: economic shortage, demand curve, supply curve, substitute goods.

"Agricultural Economics"

Objectives: To translate the results of the Russian Wheat Deal into appropriate supply and demand diagrams; to use the concepts of supply and demand elasticity to evaluate alternative farm price support programs.

Key Concepts: supply curve, demand curve, elasticity of supply, elasticity of demand, price ceiling.

"Trying to Apply a Coffee Brake"

Objective: To analyze the effect of a consumer boycott on prices in the short run and long run and to determine who might gain and lose by such an action.

Key Concept: consumer boycott.

"Price of Beer Rises at a Heady Pace"

Objective: To distinguish between a movement along the demand curve ("change in quantity demanded") and a shift in demand curve ("change in demand").

Key Concept: movement along curve vs. shift in curve.

*Instructors should consult the *Instructor's Manual* for further details. Note that, for convenience, article titles have been condensed.

"Price of Babies Rising in Wider Black Markets"
> Objective: To determine the effects of a price ceiling; to apply the tools of supply and demand to the baby market.
>
> Key Concepts: economic shortage, supply curve, demand curve, economic good.

"State Usury Statutes Fail to Restrain Rapid Rise in Loan Charges"
> Objective: To identify the implications of interest rate ceilings.
>
> Key Concepts: price ceiling, economic shortage.

"Speaking of Business: Teenage Jobs"
> Objectives: To translate various statements about the teenage labor market into appropriate supply and demand diagrams; to identify the implications of a minimum wage law.
>
> Key Concepts: demand for a factor, supply of a factor, minimum wage, elasticity of demand, elasticity of supply.

"Fare Rise Hit Buses Harder Than Subway, M.T.A. Says"
> Objectives: To apply the determinants of price elasticity of demand, by using bus vs. subway travel as an example; to apply the relationship between price elasticity of demand and total revenue.
>
> Key Concepts: price elasticity of demand, total revenue.

"Despite Fare Rise, Taxi Fleets Report New Losses Again"
> Objective: To apply the relationship between price elasticity of demand and total revenue to taxi cab demand.
>
> Key Concepts: price elasticity of demand, total revenue, perfectly inelastic demand schedule.

"Triborough Agency Cites Traffic Drop Since Toll Increase"
> Objectives: To determine the price elasticity of demand given two points on the demand curve; to apply the determinants of price elasticity of demand.
>
> Key Concept: price elasticity of demand.

II. MACROECONOMIC PRINCIPLES IN ACTION

"Forecaster Says U.S. Economy Needs $20b Boost to Avoid '77 Recession"
> Objective: To apply the simple theory of national income determination to the U.S. economy in late 1976.
>
> Key Concepts: equilibrium level of national income, government and tax multipliers, investment, marginal propensity to consume.

"It Has Been a Recession With Classic Features"
> Objectives: To apply the simple theory of national income determination to the 1974-75 recession; to determine how a tax cut will affect national income using the standard 45° line diagram; to explain how various "automatic stabilizers" operated during this recession.
>
> Key Concepts: tax cut, automatic stabilizers, aggregate demand.

"The Budget Debate"

Objectives: To determine the effects on national income of two alternative budget proposals; to apply the concept of the "balanced budget multiplier."

Key Concepts: balanced budget multiplier, government multiplier, tax multiplier.

"How The Federal Reserve Decides How Much Money to Put into the Economy"

Objectives: To calculate the maximum possible contraction or expansion of the money supply, given some initial change in the Fed's actions to buy or sell bonds; to explain the chain by which a given increase in the money supply affects output and employment and inflation.

Key Concepts: money expansion multiplier, M_1, M_2, reserve requirement, open market operation, income velocity of money.

"Tax Cut: Why it Must Be Quick and Big"

Objectives: To understand the interaction of the real (goods) sector and the money sector; to identify alternative sources of inflation and the policy implications associated with each; to provide an explanation for the "stagflation" in the U.S. in the early 1970s.

Key Concepts: demand for money, investment, demand-pull inflation, interaction of real and money sectors, "stagflation."

"Monetary Policy at the Crossroads"

Objective: To contrast the Keynesian vs. Monetarist views of the role of money in the economy and apply it to the situation in the U.S. economy in the Fall of 1977.

Key Concepts: monetary policy, demand-pull vs. cost-push inflation, interaction of real and money sectors, monetarism.

"The Great Stagflation Swamp"

Objectives: To explain the stagflation experience of the U.S. economy in the 1970s; to evaluate some recent suggestions to ease the problem of "stagflation."

Key Concepts: "stagflation," wage-price spiral, demand-pull inflation, tax relief for wage-price restraint (TIP).

"There Are Three Types of Inflation—We Have Two"

Objectives: To identify three sources of inflation and the policy implications associated with each; to explain the "stagflation" experience of the U.S. economy in the early 1970s.

Key Concepts: demand-pull inflation, wage-price spiral, commodity inflation, "stagflation."

"Ten Ways to Cut Inflation"

Objectives: To identify overly simplistic statements of the causes of inflation; to determine how various policy proposals to cure inflation would affect alternative sources of inflation.

Key Concepts: demand-pull inflation, wage-price spiral, commodity inflation.

"Strength in Wages Despite High Unemployment"
    Objectives: To determine the effect of unemployment on wage increases in the U.S. economy in the 1970s, and the policy implications of the result.
  Key Concepts: Phillips curve, inflationary expectations.

"Public Employment"
    Objectives: To analyze the monetarist view of fiscal policy and, in particular, public employment programs.
  Key Concept: fiscal policy.

"Why Inflation Persists?"
    Objective: To identify the monetarist view of the role of money in the economy, especially as money affects inflation.
  Key Concepts: M_1, M_2, "fixed rule for monetary growth."

"Steady as You Go," and "What Jimmy Should Do"
    Objective: To contrast the Monetarist and Keynesian approaches to macroeconomic policy, especially in regard to fiscal and monetary policy.
  Key Concepts: fiscal policy, monetary policy.

III. MICROECONOMIC PRINCIPLES IN ACTION

"Airline Takes the Marginal Route"
    Objective: To apply the concepts of marginal revenue and marginal cost to a profit-maximizing decision by an airline.
  Key Concepts: marginal revenue, marginal cost, average cost.

"Mink Farming Is Growing More Scarce as Costs Rise and Fur Demand Declines"
    Objective: To translate the theory of profit maximization into predictions about reactions in the competitive mink farming industry to changes in demand and factor prices, both in the short run and long run.
  Key Concepts: marginal cost, average cost, shut-down rule, economic profit, perfect competition.

"Sour Grapes"
    Objective: To apply the concept of long run entry and exit in a competitive industry.
  Key Concept: economic profit in the long run.

"Dark Days for Scotland's Own"
    Objective: To translate the theory of profit maximization into predictions about reactions in the competitive scotch industry to changes in demand, factor prices, and per unit taxes.
  Key Concepts: marginal cost, average cost, economic profit and losses.

"Lag in Tanker Business Puts the Squeeze on Builders and Owners"
    Objective: To apply the shut-down rule and demand shifts to the tanker industry.
Key Concepts: fixed vs. variable costs, shut-down rule.

"Bauxite-Producing Nations' Price Push Eases Some in Wake of Aluminum Slump"
    Objective: To identify the typical problems faced by cartels in attempting price collusion.
Key Concepts: cartel, collusion, imperfect competition.

"Copy Cat Service Tells 'Other Side' of Pricing Battle," and "The Xerox Price Story"
    Objective: To consider the issue of predatory pricing in situations of imperfect competition.
Key Concepts: predatory pricing, barriers to entry.

"Unit of R.J. Reynolds Boosts Cigaret Prices," and "Timing of Changes in Prices of 99% Plus Primary Aluminum Ingot"
    Objective: To identify price leadership and tacit collusion evidence.
Key Concept: Price leadership.

"The Declining Value of College Going"
    Objective: To use the concepts of factor market demand and supply in the markets for college and high school graduates.
Key Concepts: factor demand curve, factor supply curve.

"Housing Dispute Spurs Michigan Farmers to Switch to Machines from Migrant Help"
    Objective: To apply the "least-cost" condition for optimal combinations of factors to the agriculture industry.
Key Concepts: "least-cost condition," principle of substitution, marginal product.

"Cheap Mexican Labor Attracts U.S. Companies to Border"
    Objective: To apply the "least-cost condition" to a situation where labor prices vary due to selective minimum wage law.
Key Concepts: minimum wage, "least-cost condition," principle of substitution.

"Notes to Home Buyers: On Financing Future Schlock"
    Objective: To apply the concept of present value to a decision involving the purchase of consumer durable goods.
Key Concept: present value.

"Fast Food Chains Act to Offset the Effects of Minimum Pay Rise"
    Objective: To trace through the effects of an increase in labor costs in both the factor and product markets using the fast food industry as an example.
Key Concept: minimum wage, variable vs. fixed costs, principle of substitution, shut-down rule.

"Telephone Pricing of Directory Assistance Calls"
>Objective: To analyze the efficiency and equity considerations involved in various pricing schemes for directory assistance telephone calls.

Key Concepts: economic efficiency, marginal cost pricing.

"Nader Hits 'Violence' of Big Business"
>Objective: To recognize and evaluate solutions to the problem of externalities.

Key Concepts: external costs, external benefits, divergency between social and private cost.

"General Sales Tax Merits Attention"
>Objective: To identify the meaning of "regressive vs. Progressive" tax.

Key Concepts: incidence of a tax, regressive tax, progressive tax, sales tax.

IV. *INTERNATIONAL ECONOMICS IN ACTION*

"Trade—Expansion Act of 1962—Statement of B.C. Deuschle"
>Objectives: To identify the fallacies behind many of the more common arguments for tariff protection using testimony by a scissor manufacturer as an example; to identify the effects of inflation on exchange rates.

Key Concepts: comparative advantage, tariff, flexible vs. fixed exchange rates.

"Ford Bars Curbs on Shoe Imports"
>Objective: To identify the costs and benefits of import restrictions using the shoe industry as an example.

Key Concepts: tariffs, import quotas.

"The Nickel Peso"
>Objectives: To analyze the pros and cons of flexible vs. fixed exchange rates; to predict the consequences of currency depreciation.

Key Concepts: depreciation, fixed vs. flexible exchange rates.

"Strain on 'Snake' Eases as Central Banks Move to Prop Danish, Belgian Currencies
>Objective: To apply the supply and demand for foreign exchange to the situation in the common market in 1976.

Key Concepts: supply of foreign exchange, demand for foreign exchange, exchange rate.

PREFACE

This book is a collection of short newspaper and magazine articles that enable beginning students to apply the key principles in economics. All the articles have been used as exercises over the past several years at Harvard University and Occidental College. They have also been used in the introductory economics course in the Harvard University Extension program. Students have consistently rated the working of the exercises that accompany these articles as one of the most useful instructional devices for learning the basic principles in introductory economics.

The major purpose of the book is to help students enjoy the study of economics while they gain a better understanding of its basic principles. Overwhelming evidence shows that students in introductory economics retain little of what they learn unless they become interested enough to make use of their knowledge outside of the classroom. Hopefully, this book will enable students to apply what they have learned and, more importantly, it will give them the incentive to do so.

Economic Principles in Action is meant to accompany any of the major "Principles of Economics" texts. However, it is important to realize that it is neither a "readings" book nor a "workbook" (nor is it a study guide). It differs from the latter in that all the problems are based on actual real-world applications that are contained in the articles. It differs from the former in that the book contains very short applications that directly apply the basic principles in introductory economics. The selections are chosen so as to induce the student to apply only a small number of principles at a time. Student interest should be generated from an appreciation of the explanatory power of principles—not from the fleeting impression gained by discussions of "current issues."

HOW TO USE THE BOOK

To the Student: Since this book is not like a textbook, it requires a different approach. Before reading an article, review the questions carefully. After you have read the questions and finished the article, write out complete answers. This is important because the writing helps you to retain what you have learned.

To The Instructor: The Instructor's Manual will provide you with objectives for each article and with detailed answers to the questions. In addition, ideas on how to incorporate the various articles into your own course are outlined. Finally, a table is provided which keys each article to the relevant chapters of the major "Principles" texts.

Part I

THE BASIC TOOLS
Supply, Demand, and Elasticity in Action

Bad Business

Moonshiners in South Find Sales Are Down As Their Costs Go Up

As Number of Illegal Stills Shrinks, Revenue Agents Focus on Guns, Gambling

A Possum for Flavoring

By Jonathan Kwitny
Staff Reporter of The Wall Street Journal

My daddy, he made whiskey
My granddaddy did, too
We ain't paid no whiskey tax
Since 1792.
—from "Copper Kettle" by Albert F. Beddoe

HABERSHAM COUNTY, Ga. — When Joan Baez popularized the song "Copper Kettle" in the early 1960s, the verse quoted above described life in these North Georgia hills pretty accurately.

"There probably isn't a family around here that hasn't had at least one member involved with a still," observes Clyde Dixon, executive vice president of the Peoples Bank in Cleveland, Ga. "It hasn't been so long around here since moonshine was the only way to make money. My father made moonshine," Mr. Dixon says.

But two years ago the price of sugar—an essential ingredient in moonshine—tripled, and life in the laurel thickets changed rapidly. It takes at least 10 pounds of sugar to make a gallon of barnyard whiskey. With other inflationary factors added, moonshine that sold a few years ago for $6 a gallon at the still began pushing $15 a gallon.

At that price the moonshine market contracted severely, because for $15 plus retail markup, a customer can buy government whiskey. ("Government whiskey" is the hill country term for legal booze—stuff on which the tax has been paid. Unlike hastily made moonshine, its manufacture relies on slowly drawing natural sugars from the grain being distilled, and therefore its price is unaffected by the sugar market.)

Revenuers Look Elsewhere

The price squeeze on moonshine has forced new occupations on a lot of people who were engaged, one way or another, in what may have been, even as late as the 1950s, the largest industry in such counties as Habersham, Dawson and Gilmer. Not all of those people whose employment depended on illegal booze were moonshiners, themselves, however.

Billy Corbin is a revenue agent with the Treasury Department's Bureau of Alcohol, Tobacco and Firearms (ATF). He chased moonshiners in North Georgia for 10 years and says his team of five agents used to bust up an average of 10 stills a month. Then, in December, he was transferred to a new office with emphasis on nonwhiskey violations. "When I left (the moonshine post) it was down to no more than one still a month," Mr. Corbin says.

Mr. Corbin's boss, Bill Barbary, agent in charge of ATF's Gainesville, Ga., office, says the 108 revenue agents in Georgia used to spend 75% of their time on liquor offenses, the rest on other crimes, mostly the unlicensed sale of firearms. Now, he says, agents spend only about 25% of their time on moonshine patrol. To help fill the slack, the Treasury Department this year reassigned its gambling tax enforcement to ATF from the Internal Revenue Service.

So, for the government, one beneficial by-product of the sugar inflation and moonshine depression is an increase in arrests for firearms violations and illegal wagering. Some 15 or 20 revenue agents from the countryside were reassigned to Atlanta this spring and broke up a big numbers ring there, federal officials say; they promise to follow up with the indictment of 30 or 40 gambling operators.

The Pot Shuttle

On the other hand, with the whiskey business in turmoil, many former moonshine overlords—Mr. Barbary says most of them—have simply reapplied their resourcefulness to trafficking in other illicit goods that are still profitable. They are suspected of being responsible for the recent big increase in the airlifting of drugs, particularly marijuana, from South America to small airstrips in Georgia and neighboring moonshine states.

For example, two long-reputed North Georgia moonshine czars, Garland "Bud" Cochran and Ben Kade "Junior" Tatum, were indicted in federal court in South Carolina last summer for allegedly masterminding a DC-4 pot shuttle from Colombia. Mr. Tatum was convicted and is appealing. Mr. Cochran—who the ATF says was shipping 7,000 gallons of moonshine a month into Atlanta in trailer trucks during the 1960s—has been a fugitive since the smuggling indictment came down. Officials believe he is in South America directing more smuggling operations.

Radical as the change in North Georgia life has been since the price of sugar rose, it actually is the culmination of an evolutionary change that began in the early 1940s.

Get you a copper kettle
Get you a copper coil
Cover with new-made corn mash
And never more you'll toil.

Revenue agents agree that the old-time, 100% corn liquor made in pure copper stills—the fabled "white lightning"—was as good as or better than bonded whiskey. But when copper became scarce at the start of World War II, moonshiners turned to sheet metal vats, and in more recent times began cooling the liquor in automobile radiators instead of copper coils. The result often is a fatal dose of lead poisoning. In probably the most famous case of this, the late Fats Hardy, a Gainesville moonshine king, was sentenced to life in prison in the late 1950s after many persons died from drinking the moonshine he shipped to Atlanta.

The people who do drink it, authorities say, are almost exclusively poor, urban blacks. The biggest retail distribution centers are so-called "shot-houses," operated in private homes or stores in black neighborhoods of Atlanta, Macon and other cities throughout the Southeast. Because the price of a shot has soared to 75 cents, almost the price of safer, stronger legal bar whiskey, the ATF estimates that there are only a few hundred shot-houses in Atlanta now, down from a few thousand before the crunch.

Assistant U.S. Attorney Owen Forrester in Atlanta—who says his grandmother had a still on her land, though she didn't drink—says he doubts that even a new rise in sugar prices could wipe out moonshine entirely. "The revenue agents who work the shot-houses here tell me that there are still a lot of old-timers who like the taste of it," Mr. Forrester says. "There's a certain zang, or sizzle, going down."

How to Make It

Hill folks and revenue agents have described the methods moonshiners use to get that "zang" and "sizzle" in there.

First, there's a widespread belief, often put into practice, that horse manure added to the corn mash speeds its fermentation. In addition, sanitary conditions aren't always up to FDA standards. Mr. Dixon, the country banker, says, "I've seen a hog get in (the vat) to drink some of that slop and drown. They just take the hog out and go ahead. They can't afford to lose all that money (by throwing out the contaminated mash). I'll tell you, Jack Daniel's does it a lot cleaner." Mr. Forrester, the prosecutor, recalls a moonshiner who "put in dead possums at the end to flavor it."

Later, still other foreign matter is added. Moonshine usually is 110 proof when it's sold at the still to a "tripper," who usually is either an independent truck driver or an employe of an urban distributor. To stretch the product, the distributors usually water it down as much as 50%. Then, to make it look its original strength, they add beading oil, which simulates the swirls that alcohol makes in liquor.

If some parts of the "Copper Kettle" song were accurate once, sources here agree that one verse never was accurate:

You just lay there by the juniper
While the moon is bright
And watch them jugs a-fillin'
In the pale moonlight.

"It's damn hard work to make whiskey," Mr. Dixon says. "They have to hide the stills in laurel thickets on a mountain. You have your barrels and boxes of malt—it's corn meal mostly, some barley malt. They'll carry 200 or 300 pounds of sugar up that mountain at a time on their backs. All the time (the mash) is working it has to be stirred. That corn meal has a tendency to lump up. I've seen them get stark naked and get in there and mash it. If you don't think it's hard work, try it."

Much of the hard work, high price and poor quality is caused by the revenue agents, whose presence puts constant pressure on moonshiners to finish their work fast and get out. Moonshiners need costly sugar because they must dash off each batch of their product in about 72 hours. Bonded distillers have controlled conditions and plenty of time, so they can apply even heat as required and wait out the two weeks or so it takes to get sugar out of the natural grains.

Build you a fire with hick'ry
Hick'ry and ash and oak
Don't use no green or rotten wood
They'll get you by the smoke.

Byron Davis of Gainesville, who retired in 1968 after 31 years as a revenue agent because "it's a young man's job," says he remembers capturing a lot of moonshiners by cruising the hills looking for smoke. In fact, he attributes the switch in still materials from copper to other metals at least in part to a switch in cooking fuels from wood to butane gas. The butane largely eliminated the telltale smoke trail, he says, but didn't work well with copper equipment.

Keeping tabs on sugar sales also has helped agents to corral a few moonshiners. "One of these little country stores starts selling 500 pounds of sugar a week, you smell a rat," Mr. Corbin says.

Nowadays, however, agents say they make most of their arrests through tips from informants. Moonshiners love to tell on each other, Mr. Corbin says. Certainly the ATF needed informants 18 months ago in order to discover a fabulous 2,000-gallon-a-week underground still, which was entered by opening the trunk of an old Ford sitting in a Habersham County junkyard, and climbing down a ladder. Agents believe that the operator obtained electric power for his still by tapping into nearby underground Tennessee Valley Authority lines.

On the whole, authorities say their problem is less in catching moonshiners than in obtaining justice afterwards.

Judges and juries just "didn't consider whiskey to be a crime," Mr. Forrester recalls of his moonshine trial days. The operator of the underground still beneath the old Ford, for example, pleaded guilty and received a suspended sentence, Mr. Forrester says.

Professional

So relaxed is the atmosphere at moonshine trials that one notorious moonshiner from Adairsville, Ga., used to feel comfortable attending them. Mr. Forrester recalls, "Every term he'd come to court with mash all over his pants and listen to testimony in other cases to learn new techniques."

A typical still operation is financed and overseen by a man with substantial income from legitimate business, such as a farm or store. He hires three to six still hands and one or two women who live with them while the still is in operation, to keep house and to make the group appear to be a normal family. While the still hands sometimes wind up serving a year or two in federal prison, the boss, if convicted, usually gets probation, often impressing the judge and jury with letters of commendation from leaders in the community....

QUESTIONS

(1) In as few words as possible, and using as many diagrams as you think necessary, depict the moonshine, sugar, and government whiskey markets as well as the market for revenue agents in North Georgia. Indicate the changes in price and quantity in these markets due to the rise in sugar prices. Indicate on your diagrams which curves shift and why.

(2) The title of the article states ". . . sales are down as costs go up." If sales are defined as the total expenditure on moonshine, can you say anything about the elasticity of demand for moonshine?

(3) If the tax on Federal Whiskey was increased, how would the moonshine market be affected? If the price of tobacco rises, is the moonshine market affected? (It is, of course, quite commonly understood that North Georgians always chew tobacco while sipping moonshine). Are tobacco and whiskey complements or substitutes?

WINE TALK

First the Good News: Fine Quality Crops—
And Now the Bad: High Prices

By FRANK J. PRIAL

Some good news from France—Bordeaux, actually—and some bad news, pretty much in that order. The good news is about the weather and the bad news, of course, is about prices.

After an unpromising spring and a chilly summer, the weather in the Bordeaux wine country has made a complete turnabout. From Chateau Y'Quem in the south to Ausone in the east to Lafite, to the north, the late summer and early fall have been warm and dry.

"I've been on the phone to Bordeaux every day or two," one importer said yesterday, "and you could say the mood is euphoric."

When the vines flowered last June, the growers knew immediately that the crop would not be large. They hoped for a warm summer to produce at least top quality wines. They didn't get it. But the sun has been shining for three weeks now and although late pickings are risky — they start in Bordeaux sometime next week — expectations have soared along with the growers' spirits.

"I think we can look forward now to a very, very respectable wine," said one of the American owners of a Chateau in Graves, to the south of Bordeaux.

As for the bad news, prices continue to climb. Local retailers now have their price lists for the 1971 wines, which won't even arrive here for another two years. The wholesale quotes are double the 1970 retail prices, and 1971 was nowhere the year that 1970 was.

A case of Lafite, 1971, will cost a retailer about $400 today. By the time the stuff arrives, it could be $600, which would mean a price of about $60 a bottle to the consumer. 'Consumer' is probably the wrong word. 'Speculator' might be more accurate. While people in the trade say there are some wealthy Texans who will drink only Lafite 1959, most buyers of these fabulously expensive vintages see them as hedges against inflation.

Speaking of '59 Lafite, its price has finally broken the $1,000 mark in France. The most recent list quotes '59 Lafite at 5,400 francs a case, or $1,026 F.O.B. the Bordeaux docks. Mouton Rothschild is offered at $684, Latour at $627, Margaux at $513 and Haut Brion at $502. Lafite, 1961, is quoted at 4,800 francs, or $912.

Even in the worst of recent years, a Lafite is expensive. The 1963 is $125 in Bordeaux, the '65 is $137, and the '68 is $109.

The unexpected sunshine in Bordeaux will probably mean a better crop and a better wine, but it is unlikely to do anything for prices.

[A]

Theoretically, larger quantity drives the price down. The demand for premium Bordeaux is so great, though, that the rules of basic economics no longer apply. The 1970 vintage was the biggest in years and even veteran Bordeaux shippers assumed the prices would come in below the record 1969 levels. They didn't. They opened 50 per cent higher and within a year doubled again.

In one of the best recent articles on wine prices (Barron's, Sept. 25), Neil McInnes notes that the 1970 Chateau Beychevelle, a fourth growth from St. Julien in the Medoc, opened at $1,800 a tonneau (about 100 cases). The 1971 opened at $3,600 in January and is currently quoted at $8,400.

[B]

The irony behind these prices is that there is no shortage of wine. The famous names in Bordeaux and Burgundy make up less than one per cent of France's annual wine output and France produces perhaps 15 per cent of the world's wine.

[C]

But there is no question that the phenomenal prices these wines bring have a tendency to pull the prices of most other wines along with them. Six dollars is an extraordinary price to pay for a bottle of Chianti — until one compares it with a $12 Bordeaux.

[D]

In the same context, importers will admit privately that they peg undistinguished wines at $2.50 or $3 simply because, as one man explained: "In this market no one will believe that something selling for a buck can be any good."

EXERCISES

Passage A: Agree or disagree and elaborate on the basic economic principles involved.

Passage B: Eliminate the irony by clarifying the meaning of "shortage."

Passage C: Play the pretentious economist and summarize this whole argument in succinct technical jargon.

Passage D: Assuming the statement is correct, characterize the price elasticity of demand for undistinguished wines over the $1 to $3 range. Is this the usual case or an exception?

The Economic Problem NEWSLETTER

By ROBERT L. HEILBRONER

Vol. V, No.2   ©Prentice-Hall, Inc.   Winter 1973

AGRICULTURAL ECONOMICS

In mid-summer 1972, the Nixon Administration startled the world with the announcement that it had concluded the largest agricultural transaction in history, selling one-quarter of the American wheat crop to the Soviet government for over $1 billion. As a result, wheat prices began to soar. In mid-July when the announcement was made, wheat was selling at $1.70 a bushel. From there it climbed irregularly but irresistibly to an all-time high of $5.00 in late summer of 1973.

Charges and countercharges have since been aired in the press, anent circumstances surrounding that spectacular deal. (Consult your favorite newsmagazine for details on *that* story.) Here we are going to put to use some of the basic analytical tools of economics to help us understand how that transaction could exert so large an effect; and in doing so, we shall gain some insight into the economics of agriculture itself.

The Wheat Deal

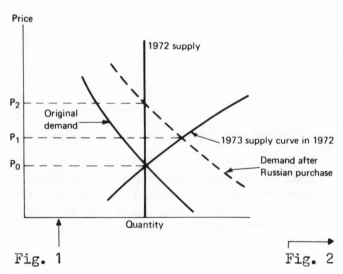

Fig. 1

The first point to grasp is that the grain crop had been completely planted and, to a substantial extent, completely harvested when the Russian sale was made. Thus the 1972 supply curve of grain was totally inelastic—vertical. As we would expect, the addition of Russian demand to American demand therefore made its effect known wholly in an increase in price, rather than in an increase in prices and quantities supplied, as Fig. 1 shows.

Notice that if the Russians had contracted to buy grain for 1973 delivery rather than for 1972 delivery, the situation would have been different. More grain would have been planted. As a result, P_1, the equilibrium price, *given a year's advance warning,* would have been considerably less than the equilibrium price, P_2, given no advance warning.

The Shift to Substitutes

But this was only the initial effect of the wheat sale. Grain is no exception to the rule that all products have substitutes. Since wheat substitutes are reasonably "close" for many purposes, the cross-elasticity of demand is high; that is, an increase in the price of one food crop, such as wheat, will cause substantial increases in the quantities demanded of other food crops, such as oats or rye or soybeans. As a result, the rise in wheat prices brought about

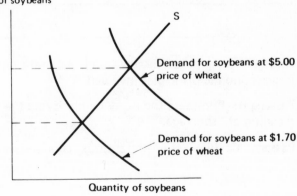

Fig. 2

an outward shift in the curve for other grain products, as Fig. 2 shows for soybeans. Thus, although the price effect of the Russian purchases was initially confined to wheat, it rapidly induced price increases among all the products that would be substituted for wheat. Together with other reasons we will discuss below, the effect was to boost the price of oats from 80¢ per bushel in July 1972 to $2.06 only 13 months later; rye from $1.01 to $3.86; soybeans from $3.50 to a peak of $12.00 (from which they have since fallen substantially).

Further Complications

We can see that the Russian wheat deal was a very important cause of the general increase in food prices. But it was not the only cause. By some curious mischance, the Humboldt current, a great Gulf-Stream-like ocean current off the west coast of South America, shifted its position in 1972, with the result that the anchovy "crop" fell alarmingly—so alarmingly, in fact, that the Peruvian government ordered a halt to all anchovy fishing, lest the anchovy breeding capacity be permanently harmed. Anchovies are much more important in world food supplies than providing the piquant touch to antipasto salads. Ground up as fish meal, they are an important element in animal feed. But once again the substitution effect was all-important. As fish-meal prices soared, there was a further induced demand for soybeans and other American feed grains as substitutes for anchovies.

Then came the devaluations of the American dollar in 1972 and 1973. Devaluation is a complicated subject into which we do not have to go here. But it is easy to see its effect on agricultural prices. Let us assume that Japanese buyers of American grains had been making their purchases at an exchange ratio of 375 yen to the dollar. For such an importer, soybeans selling at $4 per bushel would cost 1,500 yen per bushel (forgetting about transportation costs). The meaning of devaluation is that the dollar becomes cheaper: an importer can now buy an American dollar for, say, 300 yen instead of 375. A bushel of soybeans at $4 therefore costs him only 1,200 yen. As we would expect, Japanese importers increase their demand for soybeans at that price. This leads to a further induced shift in the dollar demand curve for the American crop. Because the amounts of that crop available for shipment are fixed, large increases in price result, as Fig. 3 shows.

Fig. 3

The chart shows the steady rise in soybean prices, from P_0 to P_1 as induced demands steadily shifted the demand schedule to the right.

Effects on Beef Supply

Now for the next turn of the screw. Soybeans are wanted not only for human consumption, but for animals. As a result of the increase in the price of feed grains, the cost of producing meat increases. Other things being equal, this will make ranchers less willing to supply meat: the supply curve of meat output will move to the left.

Now enters one of the peculiarities of agricultural markets. When a manufacturer wants to reduce his production, he simply fires his workers and closes his factories. But the rancher cannot fire his "workers" (really his capital), who include his cattle. To cut back on his production, a rancher must reduce the size of his breeding herd, but the only way to do so is to sell cattle that he would otherwise use for breeding. In other words, to get a long-term decrease in his breeding herd, he cannot avoid a short-term *increase* in the supply of meat brought to market. Thus the price of beef will at first go down and will rise only after breeding herds have been reduced. We see this in Fig. 4.

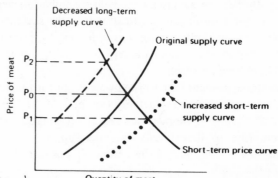

Fig. 4

This helps us understand what actually happened to beef prices. In mid-summer of 1972, Omaha steers were selling at about $37.50. A few months later, they had fallen in price to roughly $33 ($P_1$ on our diagram). Thereafter prices rose to well over $50 ($P_2$) as the supply curve moved from its temporary to its long-run position.

The Brannan Plan

The general boom in farm prices has brought an important shift in U.S. agricultural policy. Ever since the New Deal, the government has been concerned with protecting the farm against the risk of disastrous price collapses (farm incomes fell by one-third in the years 1929-1932). The means the government chose was that of price supports—a promise to buy all unsold outputs of various farm products at prices that were supposed to bring reasonable incomes to hard-pressed farmers.

Because existing prices of farm products were severely depressed, these support prices were set well above equilibrium prices. As a result, farmers could confidently grow a quantity of crops shown by OQ_1 in Fig. 5. But at the same time, consumers would buy only quantity OQ_2 at that price. A classic example of a surplus resulted.

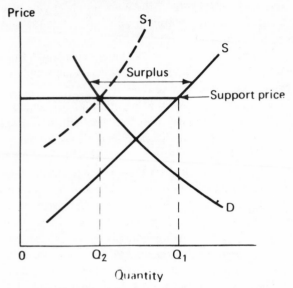

This surplus was bought and stored by the government and rapidly became a considerable political embarrassment. Therefore the government sought to reduce the surplus by imposing acreage limitations on crops, hoping to move the supply curve in Fig. 5 from S to S_1, at which point there would have been no surplus.

The strategy might have worked were it not for the huge increase in agricultural productivity (see pp. 150-51 in *The Economic Problem*). Despite the cutback on acreage, yields per acre rose so dramatically that the supply curve remained well to the right of the desired S_1 position during most of the 1950s.

The result was a transfer of income from the consumer to the farmer. Instead of paying price P_1 and buying quantity Q_1 in Fig. 6, the consumer was forced by the support price to pay price P_2 and to buy quantity Q_2. His well-being was reduced by the area represented by the shaded space.

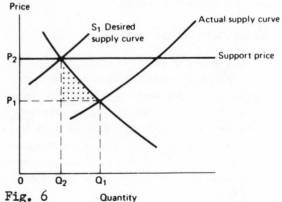

Fig. 6

Income Support

To avoid these unwanted and politically unwelcome effects, last summer the Nixon Administration finally adopted a plan that had originally been proposed in 1949 by Charles Brannan, Secretary of Agriculture under President Truman. (It was then called the "infamous" Brannan Plan.) Under the new plan the government no longer buys crops. Instead, it establishes "target prices" for most crops, *but these target prices do not affect the actual buying and selling of farm products.* Wheat, corn, soybeans, and other crops will now trade on the market for whatever price supply and demand establish. The consumer, in other words, will be able to buy his crops at price P_1 and in quantity Q_1. This means, of course, that consumers will benefit from any increases in production, which will have their normal effect of forcing prices down.

Meanwhile the farmer is also protected. If he sells his crop at a price actually below the target price established by the government, the government will send him a check for the income that he will have lost. But as long as prices are above target prices—as they are today and are likely to be for the coming year at least—he will not be able to claim any income support.

Thus the bill aims at *maximizing production.* The old restrictions on output are gone. Gone too are abuses under the crop support program that sometimes resulted in payments of over $1 million to individual farm corporations who sought to maximize income by producing as much as possible and selling it to the government. Today there is a cut-off of $20,000 per farmer. There is a possibility, of course, that there will be ways of getting around this ceiling, by parceling farms out to children or other relatives, but it is hoped that the savings will nonetheless be substantial.

Which Costs More?

But suppose that farm prices once again fall, so that market prices are below target prices. In that case there will be a transfer of income from the consumer, in his role as taxpayer, to the farmer. Will that transfer be larger or smaller than it would be under a crop support program?

Figure 7 will help answer this question.

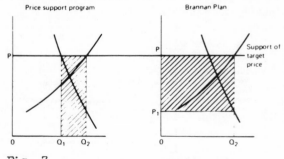

Fig. 7

Here we show two identical supply and demand curves, and a target price that is the same as the old support price. Supply and demand curves will be the same in both cases: consumers are willing and able to buy the same quantities of food, regardless of what Washington announces, and farmers will be willing and able to plant the same quantity of crops, whether they will be paid by one plan or the other. But there is a substantial difference in the effects of the two plans, nonetheless.

Look first at the panel on the left. Here the amount of surplus crop is the quantity $Q_1 Q_2$. The goverment will have to purchase this crop at the support price OP. The amount of taxes that will be transferred from the consumer to the farmer is therefore the shaded area $PO \times Q_1 Q_2$.

Now look at the figure on the right. Farmers will again plant quantity Q_2. However, the price of the crop will be determined on the marketplace. The amount of crop planted will sell at P_1, as we can see. The government will have to pay a subsidy of $P-P_1$ (the difference between the target price and the market price) times OQ_2, the amount actually sold. The tax cost is represented by the shaded area.

Which is larger, the shaded area under support prices or under the Brannan Plan? This is difficult to say, because the relative sizes of the rectangles will vary, depending on the shapes of the curves. (Try making the supply and demand curves more or less elastic, and you will see the area change in size.)

But the taxpayer is also a consumer. *The total amount of money he pays to farmers is the sum of the amount he pays to buy crops plus the amount he pays in taxes.* In both plans, that total transfer of income from consumer-taxpayer to farmer is the same—it is $OP \times OQ_2$.

He gets a different amount of food, however, at different prices under the two plans. Under crop supports he is able to consume a quantity of food equal to only OQ_1, for which he pays the high price OP. Under the Brannan Plan, he consumes a larger quantity of food, OQ_2, at a lower price, OP_1. Thus as a consumer, he must come out ahead. *He also comes out ahead as a combined consumer+taxpayer, because he gets more goods for his total payments under the target price plan than under the support price plan.*

The trouble is that we do not think of ourselves in this combined role as consumer+taxpayer *vis-à-vis* the farmer. Food prices are weighed on one scale; tax payments on another, and we do not recognize that the two scales are connected. As economists we must applaud a scheme that gives consumers more real income for their dollar of payments to the farm sector, but as political observers we must recognize that the consumer+taxpayer may not come to the same conclusion, unless he has read this *Newsletter*. Pass the word.

EXERCISE

This short article illustrates supply, demand, and elasticity in operation. As you go along, try drawing the graphs yourself. Then check yourself against Heilbroner's analysis.

PRICES

Trying to Apply a Coffee Brake

Coffee, tea or ...? That question was becoming rhetorical last week as Americans protested still another roadblock to their pursuit of happiness: the towering price of coffee. Manhattan's elegant 21 Club offers free tea to discourage diners from ordering coffee; eight blocks away, the Spindletop restaurant serves a free liqueur to coffee abstainers. Stop & Shop, a Northeastern food-store chain, posted signs in many of its 157 supermarkets urging customers to buy beverages other than coffee. In Atlanta, Store Owner Albert Solomon displayed posters saying DON'T BUY COFFEE. YOU CAN FORCE PRICES DOWN. Hartford, Conn., Mayor George Athanson, who is up for re-election this year, flagged down a city bus, jumped aboard and urged riders not to buy coffee.

So far, the protest has not reached full-fledged boycott proportions. But it may well do so if prices keep rising—and they probably will drastically shoot up in the next month or so. Last month New York City Consumer Affairs Commissioner Elinor Guggenheimer called for a nationwide one-week boycott and reduced her personal intake of coffee from 14 cups daily to none. She does not expect other coffee lovers to show the same fortitude—and is now back to two cups a day. But she does ask that they cut down: "Just pour half a cup." She has received responses from consumer activists in California, Washington, Texas and Canada. One group is organizing a coffee boycott in the Virgin Islands. Martin Rosengarten, president of Daitch-Shopwell stores in the New York City area, rigorously took up Guggenheimer's cause. He ran ads urging less coffee buying and provided a 20¢ coupon good toward purchases of tea, cocoa or hot chocolate.

The reason for this outbreak of coffee nerves is that prices about doubled during the past 18 months, forcing many dining spots to abandon 20¢ or 25¢ cups of coffee; 35¢ is now not unusual. Maxwell House, the most popular U.S. brand, sold to supermarkets for $1.46 per pound in July 1975, but is now being sold by General Foods for $2.91. Procter & Gamble, roaster of Folger's, has raised its price to $3.08.

Consumers have been protected from the full brunt of the hikes by supermarket discounting and the use of coffee as a loss leader to lure shoppers. Store brands are also slightly less expensive. But as current supplies run out, the full price will begin showing up on supermarket shelves. That could happen in three to six weeks. Says a spokesman for Sloan's Supermarkets (34 stores) in New York City: "We do not intend to subsidize the coffee companies any further. We'd like to slow down coffee sales so coffee roasters will build inventories and we will get lower prices."

Crop Killed. Why have prices gone up so much? The cost of green coffee beans began immediately rising after the devastating frost of July 1975 that killed or harmed more than half the coffee trees in Brazil, which provides about a third of the world's supply. Although the 1975 crop had already been harvested, large parts of the potential crop for this year and last were severely damaged. Brazil's production plunged from 22.2 million bags of coffee in the 1975-76 crop year to 6.4 million bags last year, a 70% drop, while world demand remained about the same. It will take until 1979 to regrow the trees into yielders of the red berries that contain green coffee beans.

Still, the shortage is more potential than actual: by dipping into stockpiles, producers have maintained high exports, and the U.S. has found almost as much coffee to import as ever. To shore up their shaky economies, however, Brazil and other coffee-producing nations have increased export taxes on beans and reaped windfalls. Brazil's tax per pound has jumped from 22¢ to 75¢; Colombia, the second largest producer, now demands $1.47 per pound in taxes. Brooklyn Democratic Congressman Frederick W. Richmond, a member of the House Agriculture Committee, charges that "this is a crisis dreamed up by coffee-exporting nations to gouge the American consumer."

How effective a boycott could be is uncertain. The hardened coffee addict is no more likely to drink tea than an alcoholic is to develop a taste for orange soda. Coffee can thus withstand price rises that most other commodities cannot. Camillo Calazans, president of the Brazilian Coffee Institute, concedes that there is a limit to what people will pay for coffee. But he does not think a U.S. boycott will seriously cut into Brazil's coffee exports—or prices.

What buyer resistance there is has not yet appreciably bitten into sales or changed coffee-drinking habits. Even at $3 per pound, home-brewed coffee still costs only about 5¢ per cup. The most effective coffee-price brake may be applied by consumers in the countries where the beans are grown. Brazil is second only to the U.S. in drinking coffee and prices have more than doubled, to $1.63 per pound, in 18 months. That may seem cheap to an American—but the average annual per capita income in Brazil is only $800.

QUESTIONS

(1) What does economic analysis have to say about the possibility of a consumer boycott successfully reducing coffee prices in the short run? In the long run?

(2) If such a boycott were organized, would you join it?

Bottoms Up!
The Price of Beer Rises at a Heady Pace, But Americans Are Thirstier Than Ever.

By DAVID P. GARINO
Staff Reporter of The Wall Street Journal

ST. LOUIS—Beer, one of the few retail bargains in recent years, is joining the inflation trend.

Confronted by unprecedented cost increases, brewers are raising prices at a heady pace. Since the first of the year, wholesale prices on the average have gone up 6.6%, and further increases are expected. In contrast, wholesale prices the previous 10 years rose at an annual average rate of less than 1.5%.

The wholesale price increases are showing up in even larger markups at the retail level. One retailer here says he's selling Budweiser and Schlitz at $1.59 for a sixpack, which is up nearly 15% from $1.39 last summer. Though beer prices vary from market to market, in part reflecting competitive pressures and varying state excise taxes, it's clear that the familiar "week-end special" 99-cent six-pack is rapidly disappearing. "More price increases will be needed," says August A Busch III, president of Anheuser-Busch Inc., the industry leader. Robeert A. Uihlein Jr., chairman and president of Jos. Schlitz Brewing Co., flatly forecasts further price increases this year.

Brewers, as well as wholesalers, have viewed the price moves anxiously, fearing a slowdown in consumption. But beer drinkers are undeterred, quenching their thirsts at a faster pace. The U.S. Brewers Association reports that first-half shipments rose 5.6% to a record 72 million barrels. Indications are that July was a banner month. Anheuser-Busch, operating seven days a week, 24 hours a day, says July was the biggest month ever. Schlitz says its July volume increased "well above 10%," and Pabst Brewing Co. volume climbed 37%. Falstaff Brewing Co. volume was up 7%.

No Deals Any More

Price promotions also have decreased significantly from last year. Eugene C. Weissman, who heads Pet Inc.'s chain of retail liquor stores, recalls that in 1973 discounts were offered with the wholesale purchase of 50 to 100 cases of beer. "Now, no one is offering us any deals," observes.

Beer companies say that not only are the price increases cost-justified, but they are long overdue. Even after brewers received Cost of Living Council permission to hike prices last year, competition restrained such action. "Brewers were getting killed by higher costs, and eventually they had to raise prices," says Donald Rice, a securities analyst at Frederick & Co. in Milwaukee. For instance, Pabst recently reported that first-half profits plumged to $6.5 million, or 71 cents a share, from $14.2 million, or $1.50 a share, the year before.

Principal cost pressures have been felt in commodities and packaging, practically cans. Barley is now approaching $4 a bushel, compared with $1.20 a year ago, with some predictions that it will reach $4.50 later this year. Thomas A. Nelson, a vice president and analyst at Robert W. Baird & Co. of Milwaukee, poïnts out, "Each crop forecast from the Depratment of Agriculture shows a downward revision. That's the stuff of which higher prices are made." Another analyst, Andrew Melnick, a vice president at Drexel, Burnham & Co. in New York, sees the crop situation contributing to still higher beer prices in 1975. "Once a crop is harvested, you have to wait till next year for any improvement," he notes. "You can't produce corn or barley from nothing."

Falstaff's "Treadmill"

On the packaging side, Falstaff has been hit with four can-price increases totaling 35% this year. "We're on a treadmill," says Ferd J. Gutting, chairman and president. "No sooner do we try to recover part of our costs with a price increase than we get another increase from our suppliers."

There are practically as many theories as there are beer drinkers to account for the strong demand even in the face of higher prices. One involves the weather. Brewers say that torrid temperatures in July boosted sales. "Mr. Sun is still our best salesman," says a spokesman for F. & M. Schaefer Co.

Another common explanation for lack of consumer resistance is that beer prices haven't gone up as fast as many others. "Beer is still a hell of a good buy," says Orion P. Burkhardt, a vice president of Anheuser-Busch. "Everything is going up at the supermarket, and consumers are much smarter than some people give them credit for. They can readily see that when cooking oil goes from 90 cents to $1.10 a bottle, that's a bigger percentage increase than when a six-pack goes from $1.49 to $1.59."

Beer executives also point out that in some markets soft drinks cost as much as or even more than beer.

In addition, the market has been broadened. In the past three years, 20 states have lowered the legal drinking age to 18 and the number of "dry" areas has been continually reduced, says Phil Katz, research vice president for the brewers association.

The College Market

Beer companies also sense that there is more interest in beer drinking on college campuses as students turn away from marijuana and hard drugs. Miller Brewing Co., a unit of Philip Morris Inc., recently appointed a manager of college marketing to push sales to students. Schaefer has shifted its advertising theme to include more young people in contemporary settings.

Even though people are buying more beer, brewers are aware there may be a price at which consumers will start to balk. "How far is up? No one knows for sure," one brewery executive says. But Jerry Steinman, who publishes a beer-industry newsletter, notes that "in some Southern states where there are high excise taxes, six-packs are selling for well over $2 and yet business is booming."

Brewers are taking some steps to offset higher costs. Anheuser-Busch has eliminated the two-day setting period in its brewing process, which the company says doesn't hinder quality but increases capacity. Falstaff in the past year has slashed $1.8 million from its marketing, administrative and general expenses. Schiltz committed $100 million for three new can plants, so that by the 1980s the company will be making 75% to 80% of its cans. Schlitz's Mr. Uihlein estimates that this will save the company $6 per thousand cans.

EXERCISE

The "Law of Demand" says that if the price goes up, quantity demanded will go down. Yet in this reading, the opposite has occurred. Are the beer-drinkers of America crazy, or is something else happening? The article suggests three reasons why the "Law of Demand" is still valid. Find them!!

Price for Babies Rising In Wider Black Market

LOS ANGELES, April 24 (AP)—Babies are being sold in a fast-growing black market that charges anywhere from $5,000 for an illegal adoption to $50,000 for a custom-made child.

Healthy white infants have become such a profitable commodity in the United States that law enforcement officials fear the Mafia will soon become involved.

"It's a racket very susceptible to organized crime," said Deputy District Attorney Richard Moss of Los Angeles. He said there already seems to be a "loosely connected organization of child traffickers cooperating with each other in transporting babies across state lines."

Some states say they are dusting off ancient antislavery statutes to combat the flourishing people trade. Others are waiting for Senator Walter F. Mondale's subcommittee on children and youth to come up with Federal legislation.

Meanwhile, baby brokers are taking advantage of gray areas and loopholes in state adoption laws. And they are profiting because the demand for a certain type of baby exceeds the supply.

"We're going through an incredible, nationwide baby hunger at a time when adoptable infants are becoming scarce," said Charlotte DeArmond of the California Children's Home Society.

There is no shortage of children as such. Illegitimate births are at an all-time high of more than 400,000 a year, and the United States Department of Health, Education and Welfare says 120,-000 children are available "for whom adoption would be best."

But they are either too old, the wrong color, or afflicted with muscular dystrophy, cerebral palsy or various psychological ailments. Selective foster parents are lining up for another kind of child: white, newborn, healthy and unwanted.

Changing social mores, improved contraceptives, liberalized abortion laws and society's fading disapproval of unwed mothers makes this child a rarity. Thus he has become a prime target of black marketeers.

"The waiting list for white babies is now three to five years, while you can get a black baby in nine months," said Mrs. DeArmond.

Joseph Reid of the Child Welfare League of America said legitimate adoption agencies simply cannot compete with unscrupulous profiteers who offer pregnant girls large sums of money and pay all the medical bills for healthy white babies.

"Potatoes or babies, whenever a shortage develops a black market is going to fill the void," he said.

Children's agency officials estimate that one baby is sold on the black market for every 20 who find a home through legal adoption procedures. Mr. Moss said Californians, who have the reputation for being trailblazers in bizarre consumer trends, have done so in the baby-selling area too.

One California mother once gave her baby to a broker for a used car, and a childless couple paid $50,000 for a baby "made to order," selecting the parents from photographs of attractive, young, single men and women in an album compiled by their lawyer.

Some lawyers have placed classified ads in California newspapers ("Young people wish to adopt baby at birth. Will pay doctor and hospital bills. Replies confidential") and others are paying finders fees to college students for every pregnant coed they find on campus.

Mr. Moss said he is keeping watch on such developments in his state; but said he is powerless to prosecute for lack of evidence.

"The mother who sells her child won't talk because she's been paid off," he said.

QUESTIONS

(1) Explain why there is a "shortage" of healthy, white babies, using supply and demand analysis.

(2) Are babies "economic" goods? Refer to this article and explain your answer.

Interest & the Law

State Usury Statutes Fail to Restrain Rapid Rise in Loan Charges

Several Legislatures Enact New Exceptions; Vermont And Maryland Lift Ceilings

Some Borrowers Shut Out

By EDWARD P. FOLDESSY
Staff Reporter of THE WALL STREET JOURNAL

NEW YORK—Tight money is above the law.

So it must seem, at least, when the law in question is a state usury law. All states except Maine, Massachusetts and New Hampshire have such laws, which set general interest-rate ceilings on loans.

These laws have produced some strange distortions in lending patterns; in New York, for instance, the usury law creates a situation in which a doctor may be able to get an auto-purchase loan that a non-doctor friend with the same finances could not. But the laws have been quite unable to prevent American interest rates in general from climbing this year to some of the highest levels in history. Most banks, for example, levy a minimum interest rate of 6½% on loans to business, even in several Eastern and Southern states where the general usury ceiling is 6%.

Cracking the Ceilings

Are the nation's lenders, then, engaged in a mass campaign of civil disobedience? Not at all. What has happened is that the Federal Reserve Board, by restricting supplies of lendable funds throughout the economy, has pushed legitimate as well as loan-shark interest rates up against the usury ceilings in many states, so that something has had to give. What has given, in most cases, has been the usury law, in these principal ways:

—Legislators in many states have riddled the usury law with so many "exceptions" that it resembles a Swiss cheese composed mostly of holes with little cheese in between. Loans to corporations are widely exempt, and so are small personal loans made by finance companies; these are generally regulated by separate laws that permit the finance companies to charge anywhere from 18% to 36% effective annual interest.

These particular exceptions are old, but state legislators have added some new ones during this year's money squeeze. Virginia, Pennsylvania and Tennessee, for instance, have enacted legislation to permit interest rates on home-mortgage loans higher than the general usury ceilings previously had allowed. A law passed yesterday by the New Jersey assembly and awaiting Gov. Hughes' signature would increase the mortgage-interest ceiling in that state to 8% from the present 6%.

—Some states have been raising the general ceilings in response to lenders' pleas. The Vermont ceiling has gone up to 6½% from 6%, and the Maryland ceiling, now 6%, goes to 8% in July. In New York, a law signed yesterday by Gov. Rockefeller empowers state regulatory authorities to raise the ceiling on most loans to individuals from the present 6% to as much as 7½%. The state's banking board announced any new ceiling would take effect July 1, following a meeting June 21 to determine what ceiling to establish.

Semantics to the Lenders' Rescue

—Where they haven't been able to get ceilings raised, lenders have shown considerable ingenuity in circumventing the usury laws by semantics. Many state-chartered banks in North Carolina and Tennessee, for instance, are adding "financing charges" or "fees" of various sorts to the 6% interest that state law limits them to on many business loans. These charges bring their effective return on such loans up to the return that nationally chartered banks, exempt from the state law, get by charging interest of 6½% or more.

In the home-mortgage field, many a lender charges a discount of 6 to 8 "points" on a loan. That is, he makes what is called a $20,000 loan at, say, 6% interest, then discounts the loan by perhaps 6%, or $1,600. In that case, he will lend only $18,400, but the borrower will repay $20,000, plus 6% interest on the $20,000 face amount. Some mortgage lenders refuse to make such loans, fearing they may violate the usury laws, but many mortgage lenders have been openly charging point discounts without running into trouble so far.

The usury laws, nevertheless, have had one major effect: They have made it next to impossible for some people to get loans. The reason: Many potential lenders who don't want to circumvent the usury laws by semantics simply won't let go of their funds—especially to would-be long-term mortgage borrowers—at the relatively low maximum interest rates the laws specify.

A Call for Abolition

This situation led Andrew F. Brimmer, a member of the Federal Reserve Board, to call last week for the "early abolition" of usury ceilings. He contended that whatever protection usury laws provide to consumers against gouging by unethical lenders will become unnecessary when the new Federal "truth-in-lending" law goes into effect next year; this law will require lenders to inform borrowers in advance of the true annual interest charge, in percentage and in dollar amount, on any loan. Meanwhile, said Mr. Brimmer, low usury ceilings "pose a serious obstacle to the functioning of mortgage markets" in many states.

Where usury laws allow, home-mortgage loans today frequently command interest of 7½% a year or so. But in 13 states, usury laws limit mortgage interest to 7% or less; in 4 states, at the moment including New Jersey and, at least until a new ceiling is established, New York, the limit is 6%.

Unwilling to make loans at these rates, or to charge point discounts, many lenders have cut back on mortgage lending in these states. They either are channeling their mortgage funds to states where a higher interest rate is allowed or investing their money in such things as bonds rather than in mortgages.

In New York, many savings banks and savings and loan associations, usually major sources of mortgage funds, are refusing to make mortgage loans to anybody except regular depositors, at least until the state's usury ceiling goes up. Others are imposing stiff conditions to discourage would-be mortgage borrowers; for instance, Bowery Savings Bank, the nation's largest mutual savings bank, recently raised its minimum down-payment requirement to 25% from 20%.

According to the Fed's Mr. Brimmer, a similar situation exists even in some states where the ceiling on mortgage loans already has been raised. Interest rates have risen to the point where they are pushing against the new ceilings, point discounts are being charged and the usury laws "are again interfering with the flow of mortgage funds," he said.

Mortgage loans, however, aren't the only kind of loans that are being restricted by the operation of usury laws. Many New York banks are refusing to make loans of more than $5,000 to individuals. State law at the moment still imposes a 6% ceiling on such loans. The banks complain it doesn't pay to lend at that rate, since they must pay as much as 6¼% (to savers who buy certificates of deposit) to get the funds to lend.

The chief victim of this situation, says Philip W. Smith, vice president of Chase Manhattan Bank, is the "man who's got a $5,000 revolving-credit arrangement with a bank and then wants to buy an automobile." Even if he hasn't used any of the revolving credit, says Mr. Smith, a car loan on top of the revolving-credit arrangement would count as a loan in excess of $5,000 and would be subject to the 6% limit.

"Business Loan" to a Doctor

Other bankers say a New York doctor might be able to get a $7,000 bank loan to buy a Cadillac. He and the bank could contend that the doctor would use the car for business, and the loan thus would be a "business loan" and exempt from the 6% ceiling. A non-doctor could get such a loan, too, if he were willing to put up negotiable collateral and have the loan made repayable on demand, rather than at a fixed maturity date; collateral loans payable on demand don't come under the 6% ceiling. But at least until the state's usury ceiling is raised, one banker says, a New Yorker who isn't a doctor, doesn't have collateral and who needs $5,000 or more can't do anything except "hope that grandpa dies and remembers him in his will."

Some North Carolinians have been able to get business loans only by changing their plans drastically. The state's usury law allows state-chartered banks to charge up to 8% on business loans, but only if they are for $30,000 or more, run for five years or longer and are made to corporations rather than to partnerships or proprietorships. Other loans are subject to a 6% ceiling, and though some state-chartered banks will make them if they can add a "financing charge," others won't.

So, say bankers, some North Carolina corporations that would really like short-term loans for less than $30,000 are applying for $30,000 loans for five years. And one banker recently told a group of businessmen who had formed a partnership to conduct a real estate venture that they would have to incorporate to get a loan. They did, but lost some tax advantages they would have enjoyed operating as a partnership according to the banker.

Margin-Loan Problems

The variations in usury laws from state to state pose a problem for Wall Street brokerage houses that have branches in several states. In New York, the "margin" loans they make to stock buyers are exempt from the present 6%

usury-law ceiling. But in some other states margin loans are still subject to ceilings of 6% or 6½%.

The brokers' general practice is to charge New York rates of 7% or more on margin loans to stock buyers anywhere and hope they aren't challenged; if they are, they will contend that the stock-buying orders are carried out in New York, wherever they originate, so New York law applies. But they make an exception for Vermont, charging only 6½% on margin loans to investors there, in accordance with the state's new usury ceiling. At Merrill Lynch, Pierce, Fenner & Smith Inc. this practice involves taking statements of account for Vermont margin borrowers out of the computer that handles other margin records and preparing the Vermont statements by hand.

Robert P. Rittereiser, head of Merrill Lynch's margin department, describes this procedure as "kind of a pain in the neck." But he's willing to put up with it because violators of Vermont's usury law can be punished, not only with fines as in most other states but with jail sentences of up to a year. "I'm willing to die for dear old Merrill Lynch," says Mr. Rittereiser, "but I'm not willing to see any of our people go to jail in Vermont."

QUESTIONS AND EXERCISES

(1) Using a simple supply and demand diagram, depict the situation in the home mortgage market.

(2) Whenever there is an "economic shortage," price no longer becomes the principal rationing device. What types of devices are being used in the various credit markets mentioned in the article?

(3) Who gains and who loses from usury laws that set interest rates below the current market price?

Speaking of Business

By LINDLEY H. CLARK JR.

Teenage Jobs

In December 1956, nearly 20 years ago, the teenage unemployment rate stood at 9.7%. That's the last time the rate has been below 10%. Last week the Labor Department reported that the September figure was about double the 1956 level.

If it weren't for the teenagers, the overall unemployment rate, a potent political issue now, would look a lot better than it does. Yet teenage unemployment remains far from perfectly understood.

William Papier, director of research and statistics for the Ohio Bureau of Employment Services, considers the matter in a recent issue of Ohio State University's Bulletin of Business Research. "The problem of unemployment among teenagers is part of the total problem of unemployment," he says. "In some ways, however, it is much more complex."

One cause has simply been a surge in the supply of teenagers. The rise in the birth rate after World War II has increased the numbers of teenagers through the 1960 and into the 1970s. The supply of young people available for jobs also has been increased in recent years by the reduction in the size of the U.S. armed forces.

Relatively more teenagers are seeking jobs, too. "The Ohio labor force aged 16 through 64 increased by only one-sixth from 1960 to 1970," Mr. Papier says. "But the teenage subgroup jumped around one-half.

"A variety of factors probably contributed to this development over the years," Mr. Papier says. "Among them, no doubt, were sharply rising living costs, the need to increase family incomes, and the attraction of statutory minimum wages.

"At the same time, however, new opportunities had developed for part-time employment — in education and recreational activities, in supermarkets, in fast-food restaurants, in shopping centers, in motels and elsewhere. Many teenagers in the labor force, it should be noted, are interested only in part-time employment."

* * *

[A]

Of course a rise in the supply of teenage job-hunters would not by itself increase teenage unemployment. Why hasn't the demand for teenagers kept pace with the supply?

"Some employers," says Mr. Papier, "after hiring teenagers have expressed dissatisfaction with their performance on the job and with their records of limited reliability and excessive absenteeism. Widespread reports of the rising incidence of alcoholism, drug abuse and delinquency among teenagers doubtless create some employer apprehension about hiring them."

In other words, some employers think that those kids are no damned good.

It's impossible to determine the exact importance of this factor, but it's surely not the major problem. In any case, it's hard to see how to deal with it either quickly or easily.

The major depressants on demand for teenage employes surely are matters of laws and rules. Some jobs require licenses which cannot be issued to anyone under 18. Laws may limit the work hours of teenagers or bar them from hazardous occupations. Work certificates are sometimes difficult to get.

In jobs where union membership is mandatory, employers may not be able to hire teenagers who cannot meet union standards. Teenagers usually are unskilled and inexperienced, and employers may be reluctant to pay them the union-negotiated starting wage.

"Another significant factor, which greatly compounds the problem of unemployment among teenagers, is that of minimum wage rates required by federal statute," Mr. Papier says. Although he says that it's impossible to measure the effect of minimum wage rates alone, a recent study published by Washington University's Center for the Study of American Business attempts to do just that.

The study, "Minimum Wage Legislation and the Youth Labor Market," is a spinoff of the doctoral dissertation produced by the author, James F. Ragan Jr., now an economist at the New York Federal Reserve Bank. His analysis leads him to some precise conclusions about the impact of the 1966 minimum wage amendments.

These amendments extended coverage of the minimum wage and provided for increases in the minimum, in five steps, between 1967 and 1971. "Had these amendments not been implemented," Mr. Ragan says, "our model indicates that youth employment would have been 320,000 persons higher in 1972 than it actually was and the aggregate youth unemployment rate would have been 3.8 percentage points lower."

* * *

The minimum wage obviously is not the whole problem. Equally obviously, it's a sizable and significant factor. Opposition to reduction in the minimum for teenagers is led by labor unions, who argue that it would merely lead to substitution of teenagers for adult workers.

This implies that an inexperienced teenager can easily replace an experienced adult, which is a little hard to accept. In any case, Mr. Papier comments that other countries long have paid teenagers less, either by law or custom, and "there is no evidence . . . that employment of adults in these countries has been negatively affected."

So when it comes to proposing measures to provide more jobs for teenagers, it's not surprising that Mr. Papier centers on a "substantial reduction of minimum wage rates for teenagers. Such a reduction, perhaps by one-fifth to one-fourth, would substitute positive for negative incentives which employers now have for hiring and training young people."

The most productive kind of vocational training is obtained on the job, and with sufficient incentive employers would provide it. There could and should be a limit to the time that employers could pay workers the subminimum wage in such a program. Mr. Papier suggests that subminimums could be used in carefully designed programs of summer employment in public parks or other recreational areas.

It's easy to underestimate the significance of teenage unemployment. A large portion of the job-seekers are still in school, many want only part-time work, and many are still living with their parents. But the social implications are considerable if frustrated teenagers grow into frustrated adults.

There should be jobs available for all those who want them, regardless of age, race or sex. If Gerald Ford or Jimmy Carter want to do something about teenage jobs, the best way to start would be do something about the minimum wage.

(1) Assume that the market for teenage labor is not subject to any minimum wage laws. Illustrate on a supply and demand diagram how each of the following events noted in the article would affect the teenage wage rate and the number of teenagers hired:

(a) Reduction in the size of the U.S. armed forces.
(b) Increased willingness of teenagers to seek jobs.
(c) Dissatisfaction with teenage workers' performance on the job.
(d) Rules that prevent teenagers from qualifying for entrance into a union.

(2) Consider paragraph A: *Even if* the demand for teenagers has not kept up with the supply, would an economist predict that this would result in increased unemployment? Explain.

(3) An economist claims that as a result of the minimum wage law (i) some workers have lost their jobs, and (ii) some new workers who would like jobs are unable to find any. How can you show the sizes of these two groups on your supply and demand diagram in question 1?

(4) How would you use the concept of "elasticity" to determine the sizes of the two groups mentioned by the economist in question 3; Explain your answer.

Fare Rise Hit Buses Harder Than Subway, M.T.A. Says

By EDWARD C. BURKS

Public buses lost one eighth of their passengers—far more than the subways—during the first full month of the new 50-cent fare compared with the same period in 1974, the Metropolitan Transportation Authority disclosed yesterday.

Comparing September, 1975, and September, 1974, the M.T.A. reported these changes on its transit and commuter facilities:

¶Bus ridership declined 12.7 per cent to 46.2 million from 53 million, an average daily loss of 225,000 riders.

¶Subway ridership declined 5.2 per cent to 79.3 million from 83.65 million, an average daily lost of 144,000 riders.

¶The Long Island Rail Road, which had a 23 per cent fare increase Sept. 1, held its own in ridership, in fact had a tiny gain; but the Penn Central Harlem and Hudson Lines, with 25 per cent fare increases Sept. 1, had a 3.9 per cent decline to 1.73 million riders from 1.8 million.

No Official Explanation

There was no official explanation of the falloff in bus ridership. Unofficially, however, M.T.A. people noted that there is a "greater element of discretion" in whether to take the bus. The bus passenger usually takes a much shorter ride than the subway rider and may elect to walk in good weather. Another theory was that subway ridership, after a steady decline for years, had almost "bottomed out" and most riders were using it to go to work or because they had to.

In raising the fare on Sept. 1, the M.T.A. had sought to soften the blow with numerous bus-to-bus transfers for an extra 25 cents. That system saves many bus riders from paying double fares. Yet the ridership ccunt plummeted.

Revenue Up 33.5 Per Cent

The increase in the transit fare from 35 to 50 cents produced a 33.5 per cent gain in subway revenue in September compared with a year ago ($38.3-million compared with $28.7-million); and an 18.4 per cent increase in bus revenue ($20.1-million compared with $17-million).

The M.T.A. also reported that Long Island Rail Road revenue was 16.3 per cent higher in September, 1975, than the year before whle ridership increased from 5,068,000 to 5,070,000.

The declines in the transit ridership figures are all the more drastic when the comparison is between September, the first full month of the new fare, and June, the last previous 30-day month.

Subway ridership was 90.6 million in June, only 79.3 million in September, and the decline amounted to 373,000 fewer daily passengers on the average.

Bus ridership (both Transit Authority and Manhattan and Bronx 6urface Transit Operating Authority) was 63.96 million in June, only 46.2 million in September. The decline amounted to 590,000 fewer daily riders.

QUESTIONS

(1) Is the demand for bus transportation elastic or inelastic over the price range in the article? How do you know?

(2) Why do you think the demand for buses is more elastic than the demand for subways?

(3) Do you think the elasticity will be greater in the long run compared to the change reported for September? Why or why not?

Despite Fare Rise, Taxi Fleets Report New Losses Again

The city's taxi fleets have found the fare increase granted last fall inadequate and are preparing to seek a new increase, according to Taxi News the industry's paper.

The 17.5 per cent fare increase that went into effect in November has produced only about a 10 to 11 per cent increase in gross revenues rather than the 17.5 per cent that the Taxi and Limousine Commission had predicted, the paper said. As a result, the paper said, the possibility of operational profit has been wiped out and losses are building up again, because "operating costs have continued to inflate."

The industry's paper said that the Metropolitan Taxicab Board of Trade, representing the city's 60 fleet owners, would probably demand that the Taxi Commission "live up to its commitment to give them the fare increase that will provide the 17.5 per cent increase in gross revenue.

"According to industry accountants, that can only be done by reshaping the fare upward to the 25 per cent schedule they originally submitted," the paper added.

The Taxi News also suggested that the industry was expected to put forward a plan to offset the rising costs of gasoline. This might take the form of charging passengers 1 cent for each 2 cents per gallon of increased gasoline costs, the paper said. If gasoline costs dropped, it said, the procedure would be reversed, and 1 cents would be taken off the trip cost for each 2-cent reduction in the cost of gasoline.

The Metropolitan Taxicab Board of Trade has called a news conference for this morning to announce details of its plans and to document the fleet industry's needs, a spokesman said.

QUESTIONS

(1) Is the demand for taxis elastic of inelastic?

(2) What was the elasticity of demand with respect to price *according to the Taxi and Limousine Corporation.*

(3) Does the MTBT agree with the Taxi and Limousine Commission about the size of the elasticity?

Triborough Agency Cites Traffic Drop Since Toll Increase

With higher tolls in effect since Sept. 1, motor-vehicle traffic at the Triborough Bridge and Tunnel Authority facilities was down by 7.8 per cent in the first three weeks of September, compared with the same period last year.

Facilities with the largest losses were the Triborough Bridge, down from 3.4 million in the 1974 period to 3 million, a loss of 11.5 per cent; and the Queens Midtown Tunnel, down from 1.36 million to 1.24 million, a decline of 8.7 per cent.

Motorists had the option of avoiding the higher 75-cent tolls at the Triborough Bridge and Queens-Midtown Tunnel by detouring over toll-free East and Harlem River bridges.

The parent Metropolitan Transportation Authority had ordered the higher tolls at the nine Triborough authority facilities to raise an extra $52 million in annual revenue to help reduce transit and commuter rail deficits.

The higher tolls amounted to an extra quarter at eight facilities and to a nickel at the Brooklyn-Battery Tunnel (which went up from 70 to 75 cents).

The Verrazano-Narrows Bridge, with a new toll of $1, had a modest drop of less than 3 per cent in traffic—from 2,390,000 last year to 2,328,000 in the three-week period this year.

The new 75 cent tolls resulted in only minimal losses at the Bronx Whitestone Bridge (a drop from 1,791,000 to 1,765,000 vehicles) and the Throgs Neck Bridge (down from 2,125,000 to 2,016,000).

The biggest loss of all—nearly 21 per cent—was at the Henry Hudson Bridge, where traffice tailed tailed off from 777,000 vehicles to 616,000.

Losses at other authority facilities were as follows: Brooklyn-Battery Tunnel, from 904,000 to 838,000; Marine Parkway Bridge, from 486,000 to 421,000; and Cross Bay Bridge, from 381,000 to 328,000.

COMMENTS AND QUESTIONS

Note the data in the table below.

Bridge	Millions of Vehicles	
	1974	1975
Triborough	3.4	3
Throgs Neck	2.1	2
Henry Hudson	0.78	0.62

As the article indicates, on September 1, 1975 tolls on some New York City bridges were increased from $.50 to $.75. As a result, traffic volume for the next three weeks was lighter than it was for the same period in 1974.

(1) Calculate the elasticity of demand for travel on each bridge.

(2) What is likely to be causing the three bridges to have different elasticities?

Part II

MACROECONOMIC PRINCIPLES IN ACTION

Forecaster says US economy needs $20b boost to avoid '77 recession

By Robert Lenzner
Globe Staff

NEW YORK — A projected slow-down in business spending next year must be counteracted by a stimulus of at least $20 billion for the American economy, a leading economic forecaster said yesterday.

"If the Carter Administration does nothing, we'll get a recession," said Otto Eckstein, a professor of economics at Harvard University and president of Data Resources Inc., a Lexington economic forecasting firm.

Eckstein, who spoke by telephone during a business trip to Minnesota, was reacting to a Commerce Department survey of capital spending that was released two days ago.

The survey showed that corporate capital spending plans for the first half would slow down sharply from 1976. These estimates, when adjusted for inflation, indicate a flat rate of fixed investment for the first six months of 1977, when measured against the current level of expenditures.

A few weeks ago, Eckstein had emphasized that the money US business planned to spend on plant and equipment was a crucial statistic for predicting the health of the economy. At that point, Eckstein believed an increase under 13 percent would mean that the moderate economic expansion of the past two months was over.

Eckstein said the economy should be stimulated by a $15 billion tax cut, which should be made permanent, direct Federal spending of $5 billion and an investment tax credit of $1 billion.

He said this package would insure economic growth of 4 percent to 5 percent next year, still less than the 6 percent rate President-elect Jimmy Carter has been promising.

"They're going to have to scramble because the earliest a tax cut can be passed is April 1," Eckstein said.

Eckstein does not think that the present Carter plan to cut taxes on a one-shot basis is sufficient to prod consumer spending.

"They think consumers will spend the whole amount, but they won't," Eckstein said. In his opinion, the tax cut should be made permanent.

The Harvard economist said not all the November economic statistics were bad, pointing to car sales and housing starts as promising.

But he added: "The Republicans made a big error thinking the economy would move on its own. There's no prospect of it straightening out by itself."

EXERCISES AND QUESTIONS

(1) Consider the following simple model of the U.S. economy:

(i) $C = 30 + 0.8 Y_d$

(ii) $T = 100$

(iii) $I = 150$

(iv) $G = 200$

(v) $Y = AD = C + I + G$

where
C = consumption (billions)
Y_d = disposable income (billions) = $Y - T$
  = income minus taxes
T = taxes (billions)
I = investment (billions)
G = government spending on goods and services (in billions)

(a) Solve for the equilibrium level of income in this model.

(b) If investment falls by $20 billion, by how much will income fall?

(c) What is the government multiplier in this economy? What is the tax multiplier?

(2) Suppose the government wants to increase income to the level that existed before the fall in investment. By how much must taxes be raised in order to achieve this level of income?

(3) Now suppose the government decides to adopt a combined policy to achieve the equilibrium level of income in question 1(a). Assume that taxes are cut by $15 billion, and government spending on goods and services is increased by $5 billion. By how much must investment increase for the government to achieve its goal?

(4) How would your answer to question 3 change if consumers decided not to spend any of the tax cut because this reduction was not "permanent"?

[23]

Normal Ups and Downs

It Has Been A Recession With Classic Features

By EDWIN L. DALE Jr.

WASHINGTON—The late, unlamented recession of 1974-75 is over: The economy has been moving up since last May. In retrospect, perhaps, the most striking feature of this recession was how classic both the decline and the recovery have been.

The recession's origins were somewhat unusual, because of the indirect effect on the economy of the explosion of world oil prices during and after the Arab oil embargo of late 1973 and early 1974. The degree of inflation that accompanied at least the early stages of the 1974-75 recession was also unusual. And it was the deepest of the six recessions since World War II.

But despite the fears of many that the world was plunging into economic catastrophe, the episode wound up being a fairly normal case history of the business cycle at work. The key to remember about the business cycle is that it is just that—a cycle. Business turns down, causing declining production and rising unemployment, and then it turns up again.

Such cycles are most easily explained by swings in inventories, or goods and materials businesses and manufacturers keep in stock. They played a typical and major role in the recent recession. Generally, because of a drop in consumer buying, sometimes for other reasons, businessmen find themselves with excess inventories. They stop ordering more goods, and their suppliers' production drops. The incomes of the workers that are laid off decline and, in the worst possible case, consumer buying drops some more and the cycle spirals downward.

More typically, inventories finally reach a satisfactory level, and ordering begins again. That is what happened this time.

In the fourth quarter of 1974, inventories were still increasing at an annual rate of $10.4 billion. Then liquidation set in, with reductions at a rate of $24.8 billion in the first quarter of 1975 and $29.6 billion in the second. Production plummeted. Just as suddenly, liquidation of inventories all but stopped in the second half of the year, and production and employment correspondingly turned upward and continued to do so in 1975. By the first quarter of 1976, a modest inventory accumulation had begun again, and was an important element in the jump in the gross national product reported last week.

Did Government policy have nothing to do with the successful recovery, then? The answer involves two different aspects of Government action.

The first are the "automatic stabilizers" that are now part of permanent law, the most important of which is unemployment compensation. Payment of some $19 billion in unemployment benefits last year was a major factor in preventing a decline in total consumer spending power. In this recession, the Government, mainly at the initiative of Congressional Democrats but with the concurrence of President Ford, extended the duration of benefits and added coverage for millions of workers.

The second are discretionary actions that are aimed directly at halting recession and promoting recovery. By far the most important in this recession was a very large tax cut, a combination of rebates on 1974 taxes and reductions in withholding in 1975. Both took effect in May 1975.

Shared 'Credit'

In this matter, political "credit" can probably be shared. After concentrating solely on reducing inflation in the months following his assumption of the Presidency in August 1974—in October he even proposed an anti-inflationary tax increase—Mr. Ford turned completely around when the evidence of deepening recession became compelling. In January 1975, he proposed a tax reduction, entirely in the form of a rebate, that would have come to $16 billion. Congress changed the procedure and enlarged the amount to $20 billion.

Did it matter all that much? Secretary of the Treasury William E. Simon has often argued in private that the low point of the recession was reached in April of last year and that an upturn was under way before the tax cut took effect in May. He does not deny, however, that the cut had an impact in spurring consumer spending, which has been the driving force for recovery so far.

Arthur M. Okun of Brookings Institution and a former chairman of the Council of Economic Advisers is convinced that the tax cut moved the inventory turnaround forward by at least three months. But he also believes that a recovery would probably have occurred without it.

The tax cut, the impact on revenues of the reduction in some incomes and corporate profits associated with the recession, and the growth in unemployment compensation and other governmental outlays combined to produce an enormous budget deficit, slightly more than $80 billion, for calendar 1975. Despite Mr. Simon's early apprehensions, the Treasury was able to borrow this huge sum with no significant impact on interest rates.

Not only did the big deficit not raise interest rates, it did not worsen inflation. By the first quarter of 1976, inflation as measured by the Consumer Price Index had dropped to an annual rate of 2.9 percent, the lowest since 1972. Declining food prices were an important element in last week's pleasant report. That decline is unlikely to continue, in part because of rising costs in the livestock markets. But even if inflation worsens a bit this year, it will remain far below the double-digit rates of 1973-74.

The recession's most painful legacy is a still-high rate of unemployment; last month 7.5 percent of the labor force. Though all measures of unemployment and production have improved significantly since last spring, the recession was so deep that it left a wide margin of unused labor and industrial capacity.

EXERCISES AND QUESTIONS

(1) Use the standard 45° line diagram to explain the causes of the recession of 1974–75.

(2) On the same diagram, explain how the tax cut of May 1975 was supposed to counter the recession.

(3) What are "automatic stabilizers"? Are they always desirable? Are they sufficient to maintain full employment?

REVIEW & OUTLOOK

The Budget Debate

A potentially instructive debate on how to stimulate the economy is taking place between President Ford and the congressional budget committees. The President wants to stimulate with lower spending and a larger tax cut. The Congress wants to stimulate with a smaller tax cut and more spending.

It may help to put some numbers on it. The President proposes a bud-taxes of $351.3 billion and borrowing of $44.5 billion. The congressional budget committees propose to spend $412.6 billion or $413.6 billion, and after quarreling with some of the President's projections, come up with roughly the same deficit as he does.

The committees say the actual spending in the President's requests is about $400 billion, which rings true but ignores that the actual spending in their own proposals will on record also be higher than the proffered numbers. They point out the economy is doing better than the President's budget predicted, and therefore tax revenues will be higher and the deficit lower. For the sake of argument and round numbers, let's say the proposals add up to the following:

FEDERAL BUDGET PROPOSALS
(billion $)

	President	Congress
Spending	400	420
Deficit	40	40
Taxes	360	380

The question on the table is: Which budget is more stimulative? At which line do you look?

If you look at the expenditure line, you have to conclude that the congressional budget is more stimulative. After all, the government is inserting an extra $20 billion into the economy. By the use of the Keynesian multiplier, you can reason that as this $20 billion is spent and respent, it grows into an additional $80 billion in GNP.

If you look at the taxing line, you have to figure the President's budget is better. After all, under the congressional budget, the government is withdrawing an extra $20 billion from the economy. This would throw into reverse the multiplier effect, if any, that applied to the spending side.

If you look at the deficit line, you have to figure the budgets are a draw, since the deficits are the same. This is the usual analysis which recognizes that an increase of $20 billion in spending would be offset by an increase of $20 billion in taxing. Under the usual analysis, only borrowed dollars carry multipliers.

The usual analysis ignores that for every borrower there is a lender. It refuses to believe, or more usually simply goes blind to, the possibility that an increase of $20 billion in spending would be offset by an increase of $20 billion in borrowing. The borrowed dollars are supposed to come out of nowhere, or out of mattresses, or out of money creation by the Federal Reserve, or out of some other place where they would never get spent unless the government borrows them.

For believing this, Lord Keynes won a title. Since some readers have recently accused us of picking on a great man, we should be more precise: He won the title for allowing his disciples to believe that. Mesmerized by equations originally drawn up under Depression conditions, they continue to believe it today in an era of computerized financial intermediation on an international scale.

Ironically, a parallel belief has hoodwinked generations of conservatives into looking at the wrong line. Believing in the godliness of balanced budgets, they also look at the deficit line. As if, for example, Great Britain could solve its economic problems by eliminating borrowing, financing solely through taxes the 60% of GNP spent by the government.

Whether or not the central economic problem of Lord Keynes' era was excessive savings, the central problem today is excessive government spending. In the ranges at which modern industrial democracy tends to operate, too much of total production is directed into less efficient outlets, and too little is left to the private sector as an incentive to produce more. The line to watch is the spending one.

President Ford is right. His budget is more stimulative. For our tastes, not stimulative enough.

QUESTIONS

(1) Which of the budgets in the table would you say is more expansionary? Why?

(2) Is it true that "Under the usual analysis only borrowed dollars carry multipliers"?

How the Federal Reserve Decides How Much Money to Put Into the Economy

By EDWIN L. DALE JR.
Special to The New York Times

WASHINGTON, May 4 — Only one thing is entirely agreed, accepted and understood about the somewhat mysterious and often controversial subject of the Government's monetary policy, which is conducted by the semi-independent Federal Reserve Board.

This is that the Fed, as it is commonly known, can create money out of thin air by writing a check on itself without any deposits to back that check. It can do so in unlimited amounts. And only it can do so — the Treasury cannot.

Yesterday, Arthur F. Burns, chairman of the Federal Reserve Board, disclosed to Congress the Fed's intentions and targets for creation of money in the year ahead. But he gave his targets in the form of range, not a precise number, and he is the first to admit that he and his colleagues are not at all certain what exactly is the "right" amont of money to create for the good of the nation's economy.

The Government's "printing press" is literally in the Bureau of Engraving and Printing, which turns out currency notes in amounts that depend on the public's demand for them. But the true printing press is a little known man named Alan R. Holmes who sits in an office in the Federal Reserve Bank of New York and decides every day, under instructions and guidelines from a powerful body of the Federal Reserve known as the Open Market Committee, how much money to create.

Orders Securities

Mr. Holmes creates money by placing an order in the money market for Treasury bills or other Government securities. He pays for them by writing a check on the Federal Reserve Bank of New York. If the order is for $100 million, an additional $100 million in cash suddenly flows into the economy, possessed originally by the people who sold the Government securities to the Fed.

Mr. Holmes can "extinguish" money, too. If he places a sell order in the market, the Fed sells securities to a money market dealer or bank and gets a check in payment. The amount of money in that check essentially vanishes. The buyer of the securities from the Fed has less cash but the Fed, in effect, tears up the check.

How much money Mr. Holmes creates makes a good deal of difference to the performance of the economy— the rate of inflation, the expansion of production and jobs, interest rates and indeed general well-being — because the amount of money affects how rapidly the wheels of the economy turn.

But what Mr. Holmes does is cause of controversy because the creation of additional money is also linked by economists to inflation. Friedrich Havek, the Pulitzer Prize-winning Austrian economist, asserts unequivocally that "inflation is at all monetary phenomenon." Mr. Hayek has innumerable followers. While other economists think his view is a little oversimplified, nearly all of them agree that "money matters."

What is more, the check that Mr. Holmes writes is only the beginning of the process of creating money. That initial $100 million starts a process by which the nation's money supply—currency plus deposits in banks —will grow not by $100 million but by some multiple of that amount.

It is at this point that things begin to get a little more complicated. In brief, the "multiplier" effect arises from the way the nation's— any advanced nation's— banking system works. It is called a "fractional reserve" system and it works this way:

Suppose that Salomon Brothers receives Mr. Holmes's check on the Federal Reserve Bank of New York and deposits it in Citibank, where deposits are now higher by $100 million.

Under the Fed's "reserve requirement" regulations, which are crucial to the multiplier process, Citibank must deposit about $15 million of this in its "reserve" account at the Fed. But then it can, and does, lend the remaining $85 million to, say, the United States Steel Corporation, which needs money to pay wages while it waits for its inventories of steel to be bought.

U.S. Steel gets the money from Citibank and deposits it at the Pittsburgh National Bank, and the multiplying process goes on. Pittsburgh National puts about $13 million in its reserve account at the Fed and uses the remaining $72 million to buy notes of the city of Boston, which deposits this income in the First National Bank of Boston.

At this point Mr. Holmes's original $100 million has already become $257 million, as follows:

¶Salomon Brothers has $100 million more cash (but correspondingly less in Treasury bills).

¶U.S. Steel has $85 million more cash (but a debt to Citibank).

¶Boston has $72 million more cash (but a debt to Pittsburgh National).

The process continues until, with a 15 percent reserve requirement, Mr. Holmes's original check for $100 million eventually adds more than $600 million to the total of bank deposits in the nation, the nation's money supply. And that money, obviously, can be and is sent to. Sometimes more spending is desirable to bring forth production and add to jobs, but by no means always.

The more money there is in circulation, the easier it is for sellers to raise prices, whether to cover higher wages and other costs or to increase profits, because customers around the nation have more to spend. When prices go up all over, this is inflation. But it is impossible to know precisely just how much money is enough or how much is too much at any given time. But there is obviously a point of "too much," as all of history teaches.

For policy makes, there are the two following questions:

¶What targets for Mr. Holmes should the Open Market Committee, which consists of the seven members of the Federal Reserve Board and the presidents of five of the twelve regional Federal Reserve banks, Establish? The relationship of the money supply to the economy at large, including inflation, is by no means clear, even to the experts.

¶Because Mr. Holmes's buying and selling affects short-term interest rates as well as the money supply, which should he concentrate on?

At bottom, the nation's central bank is controversial, and frequently unpopular, because it is a "nay-sayer." Whenever inflation rears its head, the job of the Fed is to slow the creation of money and, for a while at least, that often means higher interest rates and sometimes a cutback in production and a loss of jobs.

Switching of Funds

The right policy will always be a matter of judgment. But at the moment the problem of setting the target for Mr. Holmes is complicated by what Mr. Burns calls the "new financial technology," such as those little electronic "tellers" that many banks now make available to their depositors. Among other services, they permit immediate switching of funds from savings to checking accounts by the push of a button and even payment of some bills, such as utilities bills, directly out of savings.

The "money supply" as long defined meant currency plus checking accounts (known in the jargon as M1). There were fairly well-established relationships between the growth of M1 and the overall course of the econo-

How The Federal Reserve Board Can Create Money

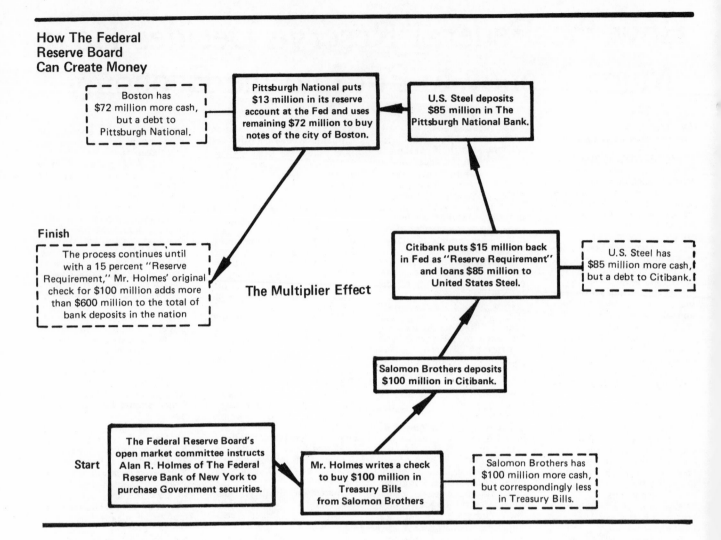

Boston has $72 million more cash, but a debt to Pittsburgh National.

Pittsburgh National puts $13 million in its reserve account at the Fed and uses remaining $72 million to buy notes of the city of Boston.

U.S. Steel deposits $85 million in The Pittsburgh National Bank.

Finish

The process continues until with a 15 percent "Reserve Requirement," Mr. Holmes' original check for $100 million adds more than $600 million to the total of bank deposits in the nation

The Multiplier Effect

Citibank puts $15 million back in Fed as "Reserve Requirement" and loans $85 million to United States Steel.

U.S. Steel has $85 million more cash, but a debt to Citibank.

Salomon Brothers deposits $100 million in Citibank.

Start

The Federal Reserve Board's open market committee instructs Alan R. Holmes of The Federal Reserve Bank of New York to purchase Government securities.

Mr. Holmes writes a check to buy $100 million in Treasury Bills from Salomon Brothers

Salomon Brothers has $100 million more cash, but correspondingly less in Treasury Bills.

Continued From First Page, Second Section

my, including the rate of inflation. But now that people, and business, too, have learned to use savings accounts as almost the equivalent of checking accounts, those relationships have gone awry.

"Our equations are all fouled up," a high Federal Reserve official concedes.

The report of the Open Market Committee on its meeting of last January disclosed that the panel, puzzled by a slow growth in money but a rapid growth in the economy, threw up its hands and simply gave Mr. Holmes an unusually wide "target range" for money growth in the period imme-

diately ahead. This meant that he was not to take any special action to create or extinguish money as long as M1 growth stayed within a very wide band.

The Fed also keeps track of and sets targets for M2, which includes savings accounts. But Mr. Holmes cannot tell when he writes one of his checks how much of the ultimate deposits will be in checking or savings accounts. Thus his art will always be imprecise and his results subject to criticism. At present, the Fed does not know whether M1 or M2 is the more important measure, though in the end it controls the growth of both.

The interest rate problem is a different one.

When Mr. Holmes inter-

venes in the market to buy or sell Government securities, he not only changes the amount of money in the economy but, unavoidably, also affects what are called "money market interest rates— the rate on very short-term instruments such as Treasury bills.

Rate on Bank Loans

The impact of his intervention decisions shows up first in the most sensitive and closely watched of all rates, called the "Federal funds" rate, which is the interest rate charged on loans from one bank to another. In daily operations some banks wind up short of their required reserve deposits with the Federal Reserve and some have an excess, and this gives rise to overnight loans from one bank to another.

Eventually, a rising prime rate brings along with it higher interest rates to ordinary consumers and other borrowers.

Sometimes, as occurred last week, Mr. Holmes is instructed to intervene in such a way as to "nudge up" the Federal funds rate himself, as a signal that the Federal Reserve feels the money supply is growing too rapidly. In either case, whether he "lets" the rate go up or pushes it up himself, the result is higher interest rates. And these days that often means a quick drop in the stock market, as happened in the last few days.

Every time Mr. Holmes writes a check he adds to bank reserves and makes the Federal funds interest rates "easier"—that is, lower, or less likely to rise.

(1) Explain how the Fed creates money when Alan Holmes "places an order in money market for Treasury Bills or other Government securities."

(2) If the order is for $100 million, what is the maximum possible expansion of the money supply, assuming a reserve requirement of 20%?

(3) Why might the expansion be less than the maximum?

(4) In what ways do you think changes in the money supply affect output, employment, and inflation?

Letters to the Editor
Tax Cut: Why it Must be Quick and Big

To the Editor:

Administration policy for copying with simultaneous inflation and recession appears to be dominated by the apprehension of Secreatry Simon and others concerning the budget deficit resulting from a substantial tax cut. They foresee the following dilemma: Either the deficits are financed by an expansion of the money supply, giving rise to future rounds of inflation; or the money supply is not increased much, and we are in for a round of tight credit and high interest rates.

This purported dilemma is an irrelevant one. Financing the additional debt does not *per se* require an expansion of the money supply since, by an accounting identity, private saving will rise by an amount equal to

[A]

the additional deficit. However, if the money supply is not allowed to rise sufficiently to meet the increased transactions requirements resulting from the larger output that the tax cut is designed to generat, then interest rates will rise. This rise would counteract the very

purpose of the tax cut. It would therefore be self-defeating to cut taxes and not let the money supply rise enough to keep interest rates low, at least for a while.

The true dilemma is between seeking an immediate recovery of output and employment through a tax cut and concomitant expansion of the money supply, or refraining from doing so for fear that a recovery might increase the rate of inflation. Under present economic conditions, with ample excess capacity and high unemployment, a recovery of output involves minimal risks of increasing inflationary pressures, while permitting the economy to continue its slide involves, with certainty, huge social costs (presently about $150 billion per annum). Furthermore, if the economy is allowed to continue its present rapid decline without a strong fiscal stimulus, the deficit may become larger than with a tax cut, because there will be a dwindling tax base, together with increased transfer payments caused by recession itself.

[B]

A very substantial part of the accelerated

inflation since 1973 is due to dollar devaluation, grain shortages, rising commodity prices and the OPEC cartel pricing of oil. Attempts to deal with this type of inflation solely by restriction of effective demand by monetary and fiscal policies resulted in extraordinarily high interest rates of mid-1974, with a full-employment budget surplus, presently about $30 billion. Thus, restrictive monetary and fiscal policies were primarily responsible, among purely domestic factors for the present recession.

Our analysis leads us strongly to recommend a larger fiscal stimulus than the Administration is now proposing, supported by the Federal Reserve with an ample supply of money, as both justified and not inflationary. Furthermore, now that the economy is showing unmistakable signs of accelerating descent into a really serious slump, the longer we wait to take vigorous stimulative measures, the larger the stimulus will have to be. It is urgent that some significant actions be taken immediately.

— Albert Ando, Lawrence Klein,
R.A. Gordon, Franco Modigliani,
Paul Samuelson, James Tobin

COMMENT AND QUESTIONS

Note first the date of this letter. At this time the economy was sliding into its worst post-World War II recession and inflation continued at relatively high rates.

(1) Refer to passage A: Explain why interest rates would rise in this case using the supply and demand for money diagram. In what sense would rising interest rates "counteract the very purpose of the tax cut"?

(2) What do the writers consider to be the major cause of the double digit inflation of 1974? Is demand pull the cause? (Refer to passage B.)

(3) After reading paragraph B, how can you explain the "stagflation" of the first half of 1975?

(4) In light of events that have occurred since the letter was written, do you agree with the authors? Why or why not?

Monetary Policy at the Crossroads

By Walter W. Heller

Arthur Burns and his Federal Reserve cohorts find themselves in an increasingly uncomfortable bind. Push by the monetarists to contain the "inflation-generating surge in money supply" has come to shove by the nonmonetarists to stem the "recovery-threatening surge in interest rates."

As the Fed funds rate rockets upward—at 5½%, this flagship short-term rate has now risen nearly two points, or about 40%, since April—the Federal Reserve's options are closing fast:

—No longer can the Fed count on rising velocity—or faster turnover of money balances associated with telephonic transfers between savings and checking accounts, NOW accounts, authorized overdrafts and other financial innovations—to stretch a 6% growth of M1, to over an 11% or 12% advance in nominal or money GNP. Indeed, during the third quarter velocity fell. No longer can it confidently count on a big yield spread between short-term and long-term interest rates to insulate the latter from the former. As the cushion between short and long rates gets water-thin, long rates are already edging up.

—Not much longer can it count on holding money market rates below Regulation Q ceiling rates on savings. Rising rates on Treasury bills and other short-term instruments threaten to lure funds away from housing-oriented thrift institutions. Disintermediation would ride again.

In other words, the rapid run-up in interest rates—more appropriate to a roaring recovery than to the muted expansion we are now experiencing—poses a threat to private capital spending. In particular, moves that boost the cost of capital funds—both directly by boosting interest rates on debt instruments and indirectly by spooking the stock market and thus raising the cost of equity funds—are anything but a tonic for private plant and equipment spending.

But the monetarists, in full cry about the inflationary evils of the 9% rate of growth in M1 in recent months, brush all this aside. Indeed, their Shadow Open Market Committee, apparently free of the doubts that assail others about the erratic behavior of money supply and the queasy course of the recovery, calls for surgery on M1. The Fed may be in a quandary as to its next move. But the Shadow knows: Cut the basic money supply by $4 billion, and be quick about it.

The Underrepresented Majority?

Monetarists are fully represented in the editorials and columns of this newspaper. So I shall not press their case further.

Rather, let me speak for the underrepresented majority, the nonmonetarists. What is their case for an accommodative Federal Reserve policy and less addiction to the money supply target?

In part it rests on the current concern over the robustness of recovery. But it goes much deeper than this. In terms of a reasonable cost-benefit test—the cost in lost jobs and output set off against the benefits in lessened inflation—the restrictive (or, at best, grudgingly expansionary) tilt of monetary policy in 1975-77 is seen as a poor bargain for the country.

The harsh discipline of weak labor and product markets, on which monetarism relies to de-escalate inflation, has given us precious little relief in the past 2½ years. Once the excess demand pressures of 1972-73 and the external shocks of 1973-74 (mainly oil and food price explosions and devaluation) worked their way through the system, the residual inflation boiled down to hard-core, Burns-resistant, cost-push pressures.

Triggered by the fierce double-digit inflation of 1973-74, annual pay increases moved into an 8% orbit, some 5% to 6%

Board of Contributors

The rapid run-up in interest rates—more appropriate to a roaring recovery than to the muted expansion we are now experiencing—poses a threat to private capital spending.

---

above productivity advances. Prices are adjusted accordingly. The upshot: a self-propelled cost-price merry-go-round that is rooted in market rigidities and excess market power and hence highly resistant to aggregative policies and overall economic slack.

To remove the structural-inflation roadblock to full employment calls for direct action to reduce cost pressures and promote competition, overcome structural unemployment, improve productivity, forestall supply shortages and bottlenecks, and, most urgently, de-escalate the price-wage spiral. Nothing in the monetarist or Federal Reserve arsenal gets at these stubborn roots of inflation. Simply putting today's economy on an extra-lean mone-

tary diet will leave the cost and supply props of inflation largely untouched, yet will hold economic expansion below its reasonable speed limits.

Referring to the institutional sources of inflation and especially to the cost-propelled inflation that "devours liquidity" and defies monetary orthodoxy, Albert Sommers of the Conference Board puts the matter both wisely and well: "Money is not the prime mover of inflation, but a link in a causal chain. No conceivable behavior of monetary authorities can hope to reach up the chain and reverse the processes of social change in which secular inflation is born."

To the extent that inflation is beyond the ready reach of monetary policy, one has to give weight to the concept of "real," or "inflation-adjusted," money supply. Dividing the increase in money supply by the increase in prices, we find the money supply lower today than five years ago. This is not to suggest that current rates of inflation should be validated or that velocity should be ignored. But it does suggest that built-in inflation consumes liquidity and that the Fed's money supply targets have to be generous enough to lubricate economic expansion as well.

In the competition between money supply and interest rates as targets of Federal Reserve policy, one should remember how volatile and unpredictable the monetary aggregates, especially M1, have been. As Federal Reserve Governor Charles Parton put it in recent testimony, they "have proved to be inherently unstable in the short run." He added that "the relationship between the various measures of monetary growth and the performance of the economy is loose and unreliable. . . ."

In other words, money demand keeps biting the hand that feeds it. Jumping this way and that—and either activating or de-activating demand deposits in the process—it makes a shambles of any near-term control, or even prediction, of money supply.

Yet those who worship at the monetary shrine faithfully turn out each Thursday to read the money supply scripture. Then, crossing themselves, they rush out to buy or sell according to this mystic sign they have just received.

The Fed Is Responsible

Much as the Fed deplores this monetary myopia in the financial community, it is in large part responsible for it. If it wishes to scotch this obsessive preoccupation with weekly ups and downs in M1 and M2, it should (1) cease its own quick markups of the Fed funds rate in response to jumps in the money supply, (2) let the financial world know that it is as concerned with interest rates as it is with money supply, and (3) publish the money supply with a clear-cut warning of its hazards to economic health: "Dangerous if inhaled or swallowed." But even that may not help—the addiction may be too strong.

This addiction has another untoward result: It diverts attention from the other causes of inflation and the measures to cope with them, as listed earlier. Worse, looking at the economy solely through the monetary prism tends to turn the world on its head.

Witness the recent article in this newspaper reporting a consensus that the Fed would not have to move toward severe restraint because slower recovery and lower inflation would "help to hold down the growth of the nation's money supply." Slow recovery—fewer jobs and less output —as such would not justify less restraint. No, indeed. Not unless it curbed money growth. The servant of policy becomes its master.

It is clear that the Fed's salad days are over. When the Open Market Committee meets next Tuesday, it will face a hard choice, implicitly if not explicitly, between money supply and interest rate targets. Mounting evidence suggests that its choice will not have much impact on inflation in a still slack economy. But it could be the margin of difference between a sustained and a fading recovery in the year ahead.

QUESTIONS

(1) Refer to the first paragraph of the article: Why do monetarists believe current increases in the money supply will cause inflation? Explain why Keynesians regard the current increasing interest rates as "recovery threatening."

(2) What solutions does Heller suggest for the "stagflation" we are experiencing? Does Heller regard the current inflation to be largely of the demand-pull or cost-push variety? Does it matter for policy proposals?

(3) Why do monetarists disagree with this prescription? What is their prescription?

The Great Stagflation Swamp

Arthur M. Okun

Speaking before the Economic Club of Chicago in October 1977, Arthur Okun warned his listeners that the following address would not send them home happy. While in his judgment the economic expansion still has a good deal of vigor and a substantial life expectancy, Okun doubted that the current strategy of economic policy will lead to a happy ending. Contending that we should not rely on more of that same strategy, Okun proposed some remedies for our economic ills, describing his message as a call for action rather than a forecast of gloom.

I N 1977, the United States will record a higher unemployment rate and a higher inflation rate than was experienced in any year between 1952 and 1972. We have not licked either of these two major problems; indeed, they have become intertwined and combined in a way that is historically unprecedented and, by the verdict of many economic textbooks, theoretically impossible. This nation has had serious inflation problems before; it has had prolonged periods of excess capacity and idle manpower before; but it has never previously faced a serious inflation problem after a prolonged period of slack.

The coexistence of stagnation and inflation or, as it has been dubbed, "stagflation," is a new problem. Yet we are dealing with it with old policies that are unlikely to solve it. The Carter administration—in this respect, like the Ford administration—is trying through traditional fiscal and monetary measures to attain both a sustained gradual recovery to full prosperity and a sustained gradual slowdown of inflation.

That strategy is not succeeding. The modest recovery targets have been attained reasonably well over the past two-and-a-half years; the economic expansion has been a rather typical, standard-sized advance. But because the recession that preceded it was double sized, it has brought us only halfway back to prosperity. Thus we have paid heavily to keep our recovery moderate, and we have had no relief from inflation during the expansion to show for these efforts.

The basic inflation rate has been stuck at 6 percent since the spring of 1975. Nor is there any basis for confidence that relief is forthcoming. Indeed, in my judgment the inflation rate is more likely to accelerate than decelerate between now and 1979, even with a continuation of a slowly recovering economy. And once it becomes undeniable that the gradualist anti-inflation strategy has failed, I fear that monetary and fiscal policy will be tightened anew to restrain the growth of the economy, thereby courting the next recession.

In my view, a serious effort to deal with inflation and slack simultaneously must go beyond traditional fiscal-monetary policies. It must invoke specific measures to hold down prices and costs in both the private and public sectors. It must break the wage-price spiral that has so firmly and stubbornly gripped the system. I believe that a number of techniques in pursuit of those objectives deserve serious consideration. Let me state emphatically that the worthy candidates do not include a return to price-wage controls, such as the Nixon administration conducted in 1971–73.

Getting Stuck in the Swamp

As an autobiographical obligation, I must record that the most recent unhappy era of our economic history began late in 1965, while I served as an adviser to President Johnson. That is when the critical decisions were made to finance the Vietnam military buildup in an inappropriate inflationary manner. But the historical record will not support any "original sin" explanation of inflation that would attribute our ills of a dozen years to that mistake. Every wartime period in American history has been marked by a severe inflation; indeed, the Vietnam episode was the least severe. But the end of every previous war was marked by the end of inflation.

The unique experience of the seventies is that the end of the war was associated with an intensification of inflation. The double-digit inflation of 1973–74 was the product of many new mistakes and misfortunes: excessive monetary and fiscal stimulus in 1972, the devaluation of the dollar, the mismanagement of U.S. grain supplies, and the OPEC shock to energy prices.

Responding to that rip-roaring inflation, the makers of monetary and fiscal policy adopted extremely restrictive measures that brought on the most severe recession since the late thirties. That recession promptly cut the inflation rate to about 6 percent by the middle of 1975. But there we have been ever since, despite massive excess supplies of idle people, machines, and plants. If our economic institutions responded currently to a slump as they did in 1922 or 1938 or 1949, the recession and prolonged slack would not only have stopped inflation in its tracks but created a wave of falling prices.

In fact, the nature of price- and wage-making has been transformed in the modern era. We live in a world dominated by cost-oriented prices and equity-oriented wages. The standard textbook view of prices adjusting promptly to equate supply and demand applies only to that small sector of the U.S. economy in which products are traded in organized auction markets. And there it works beautifully; the prices of sensitive industrial raw materials *fell* by 15 percent between May 1974 and March 1975.

Elsewhere, however, prices are set by sellers whose principal concern is to maintain customers and market share for the long run. The pricing policies designed to treat customers reasonably and maintain their loyalty in good times and bad times rely heavily on marking up some standard measure of costs. For most products, prices do not rise faster than standard costs during booms nor do they rise less rapidly than costs during slumps.

Similarly, the long-term interest of skilled workers and employers in maintaining their relationships is the key to wage decisions in both union and nonunion situations. The U.S. labor market does not resemble the Marxist model in which employers point to a long line of applicants—"the reserve army of unemployed"—and tell their current workers to take a wage cut or find themselves replaced. Employers have investments in a trained, reliable, and loyal work force. They know that if they curbed wages stringently in a slump, they would pay heavily for that strategy with swollen quit rates during the next period of prosperity. In a few areas, where jobs have a high turnover and thus employers and employees have little stake in lasting relationships, wages do respond sensitively to the level of unemployment. But in most areas, personnel policies are sensibly geared to the long run. Workers seek and generally obtain equitable treatment, and the basic test of equity is that their pay is raised in line with the pay increases of other workers in similar situations. Such a strategy introduces inertia in the rate of wage increase, creating a pattern of wages following wages.

The customer and career relationships that desensi-

tize prices and wages from the short-run pressure of excess supplies and demands have a genuine social function. They are not creations of evil monopolies but rather adaptations to a complex, interdependent economy in which customers and suppliers, workers and employers benefit greatly from continuing relationships. In general, the persistence of inflation is not a tale of villainy. By any standard, and by comparison with other industrial countries, American unions have been remarkably self-restrained in recent years. Business, meanwhile, has kept its markups below levels that would be justified by the current cost of capital.

In combination, business and labor have been raising prices about 6 percent a year and increasing hourly compensation (wages, private fringe benefits, and employers' payroll tax costs) by about 8 percent a year. The 8-and-6 combination allows a typical margin of real wage gains in line with the normal trend of productivity. Precisely for that reason, it becomes self-perpetuating. New wage decisions are made against the background of 8 percent advances in other wages and 6 percent increases in prices. And so they tend to center on 8 percent. Then, with hourly labor costs rising by 8 percent, businesses find their labor costs per unit of output up about 6 percent, and so their prices continue to rise by 6 percent.

There is no handle on either the wage side or the price side by which we can pull ourselves out of this stagflation swamp. Nor can any single industry or union provide a handle, except by making an unreasonable sacrifice of its own self-interest. It must do what everybody else is doing in order to protect itself. Analogously, if all the spectators at a parade are standing on tiptoe in an effort to get a better view, no individual can afford to get off his uncomfortable tiptoe stance. Ending the discomfort requires a collective decision.

Production and Jobs

Because prices and wages respond only a little to changes in total spending, production and employment respond a lot. And that is the fundamental limitation of fiscal and monetary restraints as a means of curbing inflation. Those policies clearly can put the lid on total spending for goods and services. The holddown in total spending is then split between a cutback in production and a slowing of inflation. But that "split" is the result of price and wage determination; it is not controlled by Washington. We learned—or should have learned—in the past three years that the split is extremely unfavorable. The reaction to weaker markets is loaded with layoffs, no-help-wanted signs, cutbacks of production schedules, and slashes in capital budgets. At most, it is sprinkled with holddowns in prices and wages. To save one percentage point on the basic inflation rate through policies that restrain total spending, we lose more than five points—easily $100 billion—of our annual real GNP.

The recession and slack of 1974–77 have exacted a toll of $500 billion in lost production of capital goods and consumer goods that could have added to our productivity and our standard of living. That cost should

---

"We cannot count on our current policies to pull us out of the stagflation swamp. The evidence of recent years has accumulated and become overwhelming. The time has come to face the likelihood that we have a losing hand, and to deal a new one."

---

be clearly recognized, although it must be equally recognized that there was, and is, no toll-free route of escape from our problems. In fact, the toll keeps mounting. After thirty months of economic expansion, we have moved only about half the distance from the depths of the recession to a reasonable and feasible level of prosperity or full employment. Serious statistical studies designed to estimate the unemployment rate associated with reasonably balanced—neither slack nor tight—labor markets converge on a range between 5 and 5.5 percent. They demonstrate that with today's structure of labor markets, full employment certainly cannot be defined as a 4 percent unemployment rate. But neither can it be pegged anywhere near our recent 7.1 percent. Since unemployment has come down from 9 percent at the worst of the recession to 7.1 percent, we are about halfway to a reasonable cyclical target in the zone of 5 to 5.5 percent.

The excess of nearly two percentage points in the unemployment rate is not a structural phenomenon; it is not concentrated in "unemployables," secondary workers, or groups especially affected by government benefit programs. It is instructive to compare the unemployment rates of eminently employable groups today with their 1973–74 average:

	August 1977	1973–74 Average
	(percent)	
Married men	3.5	2.5
Craftsmen	5.5	4.0
Factory workers	7.0	5.0
"Job losers"	3.4	2.1
	(weeks)	
Average duration of unemployment	13.5	9.8

Unemployment remains high because production has not grown enough to generate the jobs required to get us back to prosperity. The behavior of the unemployment rate in recent years poses no mystery. Indeed, it has moved remarkably true to form in relation to the growth of production. Between 1973 and 1977, our annual growth rate has averaged 2 percent, and such a substandard growth performance entails a much increased rate of unemployment. Economists can disagree about whether the nation's "potential growth rate"— the rate of growth of real GNP that maintains a constant unemployment rate—is as low as 3.3 percent or as high as 4 percent, but it surely is not 2 percent. If I use my favorite number, 3.75 percent, for the potential growth rate, the 2 percent average actual growth rate since 1973 would be expected to raise the unemployment rate by 2.3 percentage points, in line with a rule-of-thumb formula that I developed in 1961. That would point to an unemployment rate a little above 7 percent currently, and that is where we are.

The potential growth rate of the economy is influenced by trends in productivity and in labor force participation. In the seventies, a rising fraction of women and young people have chosen to enter the labor force. That increase in "work ethic" permits the economy to enjoy greater growth without encountering tight labor markets. Indeed, in its absence, the rather disappointing trend in productivity would have significantly lowered our trend of potential growth. To be sure, if women and teenagers stopped hunting for jobs and went back to their knitting and ball-playing, respectively, our unemployment figures would be lower. But our labor markets would be tighter, and the potential of the economy would be reduced. The increased labor force participation of these workers is correctly viewed as an opportunity and not as a burden.

At the level required to bring the unemployment rate down to the middle of the 5-to-5.5 zone, our real GNP would be about $100 billion, or 5.5 percent, above its present level. The evidence suggests that our plant capacity could accommodate that extra output without strain, so long as it was broadly spread across sectors. Such a judgment must rest on estimates of operating rates, which are admittedly imperfect. But they are not likely to be seriously biased, either upward or downward. The estimate of capacity may inappropriately include some outmoded facilities, but it is just as likely to omit some rehabilitated facilities.

In short, idle resources and sacrificed output continue to represent an enormous national extravagance. Economists ought to be devoting more of their efforts and ingenuity to correcting that waste and less to talking it away or defining it out of existence.

The Costs of Inflation

Just as 7 percent unemployment is not full employment, so 6 percent inflation is not price stability. For the past two years, inflation has been reasonably steady and relatively well predicted, yet it remains domestic Public Enemy No. 1 in the view of a majority of the American people. I find that entirely understandable. In a system that rests on the dollar as a yardstick, a score-keeping device, and a basis for planning and budgeting, the instability of the price level adds enormously to uncertainty and risk.

In our institutional environment, most people cannot hedge their wealth or their incomes against inflation. The single-family home has been the only major asset that has served as an effective inflation hedge during the past decade; and it obviously is not a feasible outlet for steady flows of saving. Common stocks have been miserable failures as inflation hedges; savings deposits and life insurance offer no effective inflation protection. A small minority of Americans have obtained cost-of-living escalators that effectively protect their real incomes against inflation. But their escalated wages are passed through into prices and thereby destabilize the real incomes of the majority whose earnings are not indexed. Escalators are a means of passing the buck among groups within our society, not of protecting the buck for the whole of society.

This country has not adapted, and is not adapting, to 6 percent inflation. The tolerable rate of inflation in this society is considerably below 6 percent. In the early sixties, 1.5 percent inflation was generally regarded as tolerable; in the early seventies, a 3 percent rate was widely accepted. If we were now to label 6 percent inflation as acceptable, who could believe that such a decision was the final turn of the ratchet? This country needs an effort to restore the reliability of the dollar, not a set of innovations to replace it; it needs an effort to curb inflation, not a program to learn to live with it.

With current prospects and policies, the basic inflation rate is not likely to drop below 6 percent during the remainder of the present economic expansion. To be sure, the inflation rate fluctuates from quarter to quarter, and minor wiggles and jiggles tend to generate vain hopes and groundless fears. Recent declines in farm prices and a downward blip in mortgage interest rates have generated favorable news. That is genuinely reassuring evidence that the jump in inflation to an 8 percent rate earlier this year was transitory. But the latest figures do not signify a fundamental improvement that is likely to be sustained.

Our chance for some net relief from inflation has been reduced by a new wave of congressional actions that add to particular costs and prices. Employers' hourly labor costs will be raised by hikes in payroll taxes in January 1978 for both social security and unemployment insurance. Further increases in payroll taxes are contemplated to finance proposed reforms of social security. The minimum wage seems slated to move up from $2.30 to $2.65. The first installment of the wellhead tax on crude oil is scheduled to take effect in 1978. Government farm programs have reinstituted acreage cutbacks, deliberately reducing the productivity of our agriculture. Many of these cost-raising measures have some justification. No one of them spells the difference between price stability and rampant inflation. But, in combination, they may well add 1.5 percent to the inflation rate by late 1978.

This wave of cost-raising measures deserves far more attention and scrutiny than it has received. Reliance on such measures is nothing new, but their total magnitude does set a new record. The Congress may have been tempted to load costs on the budgets of consumers and employers in order to avoid loading more onto the federal budget. In several of these areas, the President initially advanced proposals that were admirably restrained, but then compromised in the face of strong political opposition. (When some of the press welcomes such instances as evidence of the President's education in the ways of Washington, I cannot share the enthusiasm.) Meanwhile, the financial and business community has been so preoccupied with Thursday afternoon reports on the money supply and reestimates of the federal deficit that it has missed the big new inflationary game in town.

All things considered, my best guess is that between now and 1979, inflation is more likely to accelerate than to decelerate—and not because of overly rapid growth or excess demand.

With that inflation forecast, a good growth performance in 1979 and 1980 seems unlikely. Bad news on inflation would turn into bad news for prosperity in several ways. First, it would mean higher interest rates. Short-term interest rates cannot responsibly be held below the inflation rate indefinitely. To me, an interest rate on Treasury bills above 7 percent would sound an alarm; it would lead to disintermediation and create a mortgage famine that would starve homebuilding. Second, in an environment of stubborn and intensifying inflation, the makers of fiscal policy would be understandably reluctant to provide any stimulus to the investor or consumer that might be needed to sustain growth. Third, bad news on inflation would heighten consumer anxiety and once again weaken discretionary household spending.

The connection between worsening inflation and a subsequent recession is not magic or automatic, but it is genuinely built into the attitudes and expectations of our public and our policymakers. "Inflation backlash" is a reality. Given that reality, we simply cannot take the risk of doing what comes naturally and hoping for good luck.

Thus, my principal message is that we cannot count on our current policies to pull us out of the stagflation swamp. The evidence based on the experience of recent years has accumulated and become overwhelming. "Patience and fortitude" is no longer an acceptable response to our disappointments. The time has come to face the likelihood that we have a losing hand, and to deal a new one.

A Fiscal-Monetary Cure?

Some who accept my grim verdict about current policies call for a new monetary-fiscal strategy. And they point in opposite directions. On one side, the argument takes these lines. If a slack economy is not curing inflation, then why take the high costs of slack? Why not try to grow out of the inflation with stimuli, such as large permanent tax cuts backed up by a monetary policy committed to low interest rates, that have reliably spurred growth every time they have been applied in the past?

On the other side, the reverse case is made. If inflation is not abating with 5 percent real growth, isn't it clear that we need more restrictive policies to slow the economy down until inflation responds?

These polar-opposite proposals have in common the justified anxiety that our current act of juggling two eggs may lead to both getting broken. But I fear that they have one other thing in common that is less admirable. They are asking us to kid ourselves. The expansionists are right in that production and jobs are good things—but not because they alleviate inflation. Any major stimulative strategy, taken alone, will hasten the day that inflation accelerates and that inflation backlash sets in. The restrictionists are right in that a big enough dose of restraint would curb inflation—but only at the price of some $100 billion in output per point of inflation reduction.

Some groups in the business and financial community no doubt would applaud a hypothetical announcement that the government was cutting its spending by, say, $30 billion and that the Federal Reserve was now setting monetary targets aimed at, say, only 7 percent growth of nominal GNP. But when government contracts were rescinded, when banks began closing loan windows, when cash registers stopped ringing, the responses would be entirely predictable: new waves of layoffs, new slashes in capital budgets, a collapse in productivity, and new demands that the government stop imports, shorten workweeks, and launch programs of makework jobs.

Perhaps the most appealing variant of the restraint prescription is the call for a *very gradual*, but consistently maintained, slowing of monetary growth and reversal of fiscal stimulus. As far as I can see, that strategy —taken alone—offers us a long, dull headache instead of a short, severe one, but no smaller total amount of pain. Moreover, its plan to curb demand gently enough to avoid a recession surely sets a new record for fine-tuning. It reminds me of the story about the Greek boy who thought he could pick up a full-grown bull if he started with a newborn calf and lifted it every day. The first little trimming of total demand is a mere baby calf. It would not do production and employment much harm (nor would it do our inflation performance much good). But, as time progressed, that calf would grow into a bull —and we could not count on lifting it.

A Program for Prosperity and Price Stability

We need an anti-inflation program that is not an anti-growth program, and that goes beyond traditional fiscal and monetary measures. In the past three years, I have assembled long menus of measures that might hold down costs and prices without holding down production and employment. Now I offer a specific set of proposals. I do so uncomfortably—I left the business of packaging four-point programs nearly a decade ago, and I prefer to stay out of it. I do so diffidently—because the facets of the program have not been polished by staff work or constructive criticism. But I do so enthusiastically because I am convinced that the general approach it embodies represents our best hope for getting out of the stagflation swamp.

No net federal cost-raising. First, the administration should set a target of zero net cost-raising measures for 1978, and should report quarterly to the American people on the achievement of that target. Any new cost-raising governmental action that imposed higher labor costs on employers or higher prices on consumers would have to be neutralized by a federal cost-reducing measure—lightening the burden of regulation or providing a cost-cutting subsidy. Thus we would be insured against an encore of the cost-raising actions of 1977.

Sales tax–cut incentive. Second, the federal government should institute a grant-in-aid program that would defray half the revenue loss of any state or city that reduced or repealed its sales taxes during 1978. Mayors and governors obtaining federal aid for sales tax cuts would pledge not to increase other cost-raising taxes during the period (but could raise income taxes). An allocation of $6 billion of federal outlays for this program would fund a 1 percentage point cut in the consumer price index. Sales taxes are part of the cost of living, both genuinely and statistically. Reductions in those taxes would hold down consumer prices and have anti-inflationary effects on wages that are linked, formally or informally, to the cost of living.

Tax relief for price-wage restraint. Third, a tax relief incentive should be offered to workers and businessmen who enlist in a cooperative anti-inflationary effort. To qualify for participation, a firm would have to pledge, at the beginning of 1978, to hold its employees' average rate of wage increase below 6 percent and its average rate of price increase below 4 percent (apart from a dollars-and-cents passthrough of any increases in costs of materials and supplies) during the course of the year. In return for participation, employees of the firm would receive a tax rebate (generally through withholding) equal to 1.5 percent of their wage or salary incomes with a ceiling of $225 per person; the firm would receive a 5 percent rebate on its income tax liabilities on domestic operating profits.

Any firm covered by a collective bargaining contract would be obliged to consult with union representatives before deciding to participate in the program. Typical workers who were counting on before-tax wage increases of 8 percent or less would benefit from participation.

I would hope for strong moral suasion, led by the President himself, to enlist participants in the program. But nonparticipation would be a matter of free choice and not subject to penalty. At the end of the year, each participating firm would file a statement of compliance that would be subject to audit by the Internal Revenue Service.

The total cost in federal revenues of the cooperative restraint program might approach $15 billion; with the sales tax grants, it could total $20 billion. Tax cuts of that magnitude are being widely espoused in the context of the forthcoming tax reform program. I would postpone the tax cuts in the reform package in the conviction that a pro-growth, anti-inflation program deserves a more urgent priority on the nation's agenda.

Obviously, the increase in purchasing power and profitability provided by the anti-inflationary tax cuts would stimulate consumption and investment. Indeed, the prospect of a credible attack on inflation could reduce the uncertainty that now constricts capital budgeting. If the program achieved its objective of a mutual and balanced de-escalation of wages and prices, there would be no overhang of "catch-up" wage and price increases in 1979. But opportunities should be held open for renewing the program (or phasing it out more gradually) in an effort to cut inflation once again.

New GNP targets. Fourth and finally, the administration and the Federal Reserve in cooperation should set forth revised fiscal and monetary targets designed to ensure full recovery *and* lower inflation. For 1978 those targets should aim for an encore of the increase in *nominal* GNP of 1977—about 10.5 percent—with more real growth and less inflation. For 1979 and 1980 they should aim to bring the growth of nominal GNP progressively into single-digit territory. Thus they will call for declining federal deficits and slowing money growth (appropriately adjusting for any further significant shifts in velocity). Such a fiscal-monetary strategy should strongly reinforce the credibility of the anti-inflation program and help to ensure that we don't slide back into the swamp.

Still, the first requirement is to get out of the swamp. My program is neither a panacea nor a long-run insurance policy against inflation and stagflation. But its approach offers a good chance of bringing about a mutual de-escalation of prices and wages, and an end to the insidious wave of governmental cost-raising actions. It recognizes that traditional monetary-fiscal policies are powerful tools to promote full recovery and to prevent a resurgence of excess-demand inflation. But it also recognizes realistically that they cannot by themselves cure stagflation. That new problem requires the additional help of new remedies, which of necessity are unconventional and unproved. Whether the new remedies become politically feasible will depend on whether knowledgeable Americans face up to the reality that we are likely to remain stuck in the stagflation swamp with current policies, and whether they are willing to consider seriously—and to criticize constructively—alternative routes to noninflationary prosperity.

QUESTIONS

(1) From your reading of the article, indicate why Okun believes that fiscal and monetary policies have failed in the recent past to solve the "stagflation" problem?

(2) What alternatives does he propose?

There Are Three Types of Inflation; We Have Two

BY JAMES TOBIN

NEW HAVEN, Conn.—Three decades of experience tell us that inflation is endemic to modern democratic industrial societies. Fortunately the same record indicates that these economies are nonetheless capable of yielding their citizens substantial gains in well-being decade after decade. But hysteria about inflation may lead to policies that keep economic progress well below its potential.

The United States inflation of 1973-74 is a complex and difficult case, unique in our history. In general we may distinguish three types of inflation: a) excess demand inflation, popularly summarized as "too much money chasing too few goods," b) the wage-price-wage spiral, and c) shortages and price increases in important commodities. Our current inflation is a combination of b) and c). But public discussion generally ignores these distinctions and identifies every inflation, including the present case, as the classical type a). From this diagnosis, mistaken in my opinion, follows the classical remedy, the "old-time religion" of restricting aggregate demand by tight monetary policy and by fiscal austerity.

With some oversimplification, we can say that the U.S. suffered a severe case of excess-demand inflation a) in 1966, when President Johnson and Secretary of Defense Robert McNamara piled war demands onto an economy already operating close to its capacity, and ignored their economists' pleas to raise taxes. Re-enforced by a lesser dose of excess demand in 1968, the 1966 outburst left in its wake a surprisingly stubborn case of inflation type b), the wage-price-wage spiral. Attaining a momentum of its own, this inflation first accelerated and then abated somewhat under the deliberately recessionary policy of 1969-71, assisted by Phases I and II of the controls introduced in August 1971.

At the end of 1972 the ongoing wage-price dynamic was producing over-all inflation of 3½ per cent per year, down from 5 per cent in 1969 and 1970. However, it was obvious, as events confirmed, that some of the improvement was transient window dressing which would not survive relaxation of controls and completion of the recovery from recession.

Some observers view the 1973 expansion of the American economy as another case of excess demand and blame the Federal Reserve and the Nixon budget for overheating the economy once again. But unemployment never fell below 4.6 per cent, and the Government cooled off the boom pretty quickly after midyear. In any case, the underlying wage-price-wage dynamic was proceeding at year-end with wage increases of 7 to 8 per cent, which with normal productivity gains would mean price inflation in the neighborhood of 5 per cent per year.

■

But meanwhile the United States was hit by a severe type c) inflation, a spectacular increase in commodity prices. For the first time since the Korean war, external events sharply increased the prices facing American producers and consumers. Everyone knows about the world shortages of food and energy, and about the aggressive new policies of the oil-producing nations, who have in effect imposed an excise tax of $10 to $15-billion a year on American consumers of their products. What may be less well understood is the role of the 16 per cent depreciation of the dollar in foreign exchange since 1970. Working precisely as the architects of the policy hoped, dollar depreciation made imports about $10 billion a year more expensive to Americans. Combined with booms in Europe and Japan, depreciation also increased foreign demand for U.S. products, notably basic agricultural and industrial commotities. Foreign demands for our exports created shortages and price increases for American buyers.

Now there are two important differences between types b) and c) inflation. First, the wage-price-wage spiral keeps going of its own momentum. Wage increases are covered by price boosts, and subsequent wage settlements respond both to past wage patterns and to price inflation. The type c) commodity price increases, however, are once-for-all adjustments to new supply-demand situations: those prices won't necessarily fall, but all that is needed to improve the rate of inflation is that they stop rising.

Second, the wage-price-wage spiral does not of itself impose any collective loss on the nation or on the urban nonagricultural sector of the economy in which it occurs. One man's price is another's income; when buyers pay more, sellers receive more. The inflation may proceed unevenly, so that some workers, consumers, and property owners lose while others gain; such relative distributional changes are always occurring, inflation or no inflation. But it is simply vulgar nonsense—no less for constant repetition by economists, politicians, bankers, and journalists—to say that an internal self-contained inflation causes per se a loss of economic welfare in aggregate.

The commodity price increases are a different matter. They are symptoms of a real national economic loss, and in particular a loss to urban wage-earners and consumers. In current circumstances, we are paying more for oil and other imports. We're not just paying more dollars but more work and resources; under our new foreign exchange rate policy we can no longer buy foreign goods with paper dollars i.o.u.'s. We are also paying more, about $25 billion a year gross, to our own farmers. Recorded declines of real wages are the painful and unavoidable consequences. To attribute them indiscriminately to "inflation" is superficial and misleading.

■

The economy is currently in recession, and the prospects are for abnormally slow growth in output and for rising unemployment. The Federal Reserve is administering the classical medicine for excess demand inflation a), because that is the only medicine it has. Some of its spokesmen, supporters, and critics regard every inflation, almost by definition, as the excess demand type—on the ground that, whatever the proximate origins of inflation, it could be avoided by sufficiently resolute restriction of demand. The idea is that the wage-price-wage spiral will unwind if enough slack—idle capacity and unemployment—is created. Extreme advocates of the old-time religion even argue that determined disinflation of demand could have yielded big enough reductions in prices of other goods and services to offset or average out the recent price increases of food, fuel and basic materials.

The trouble with this prescription is that it will not succeed without years of economic stagnation, high unemployment, and lost production, with much more severe consequences for real economic welfare than the inflation itself. Experience shows that the wage-price-wage spiral is extremely resistant to unemployment, recession, and economic slack. The unpleasant fact of life is that the wage- and price-setting institutions of our economy, and of every other non-Communist economy, are biased toward inflation. Wages and prices rise when and where demand is strong much more readily than they decline when and where demand is weak. While the classical medicine would have prevented the Vietnam burst of inflation, it will take much more time and pain than its advocates admit to overcome the wage-price-wage inflation now built into our economy.

The main inflationary threat this year is that the temporary inflation of type c) will be permanently built into the ongoing wage-price-wage spiral. The setbacks to real wages reflected in higher prices of food, fuel, and other commodities cannot really be reversed. General attempts to "catch up" by escalated wage settlements will simply be defeated by accelerated price inflation. So Washington is right to be alarmed by this year's wage settlements.

But there is very little the Federal Reserve can do about them, even if the Fed provokes a full-blown recession. The settlements are already in the works, and they depend much more on the recent history of wages and prices than on the current strength or weakness of demand. The budget-makers of the Executive and the Congress are in much the same position. They too can be nobly and resolutely austere, pretending they are fighting a classical type (a) inflation. But the results of budget cutting will be measured more in lower unemployment and production statistics than in wages and prices. Present anti-inflation hysteria may well yield policies that bring us the worst of several worlds.

Is there a more promising and less costly way to confront the unique inflationary problem of 1974? If ever there was a time for what the Europeans call "incomes policy," the time is now. It may be that the Nixon experiment with wage and price controls was never a good idea, and the stop-and-go alternation of phases certainly didn't help. But the total abandonment, in April of this year, of every legal or informal restraint was incredibly untimely.

∎

What was needed was Presidential leadership—in open, candid understanding with business, labor, agriculture, and consumers—to establish realistic moderate guideposts for wages and prices. We still need what some of us have called a new social contract for the economy, along the following lines: (1) Monetary and fiscal policy would be geared, not to increase unemployment, but to keep it from rising, and to achieve, not to thwart, the 4 per cent a year growth in production of which our economy is capable. (2) Workers' take-home pay would be increased by cutting Social Security payroll taxes and by making the structure of those taxes more equitable and progressive. This tax cut would provide part of the demand stimulus needed under (1). (3) Labor, for its part, would consent to a general wage guidepost of 8 or 9 per cent and Washington would expect and exact comparable moderation in business and agricultural price-setting.

The hour is late. But the long national nightmare is over. Our new President has the trust and goodwill of the American people. If the economic problem he confronts is unique, he also enjoys a unique opportunity to seek a new direction.

QUESTIONS

(1) What are the three types of inflation, according to Tobin?

(2) Which of the three were at work at the time Tobin was writing? (To refresh your memory, see the second paragraph of this article.)

(3) In retrospect, do you think Tobin was correct in this analysis?

Ten Ways to Cut Inflation

The most distressing thing about last week's news that consumer prices swelled at a 7.4% annual rate in February was that Washington's policymakers were relieved. They had expected the rise to be worse. Indeed, many of them take high inflation for granted, which is the first step toward giving up the fight. They forget too easily that not too long ago 3% inflation was considered to be steep, 4% dangerous, 5% intolerable. Now experts chorus that the U.S. has an "underlying" inflation rate of at least 6%—intractable, indomitable, unassailable.

[A]

In fact, the inflation rate can—and must—be brought down. There is no mystery about what causes inflation: too many demands by too many people upon a limited amount of national wealth. The cure is more difficult to prescribe, but surely it involves discipline, limits, sacrifice. The means to retard inflation are economically feasible, but they are thought to be politically impractical. We know many of the ways; all we lack is the will.

The will is notably absent during election year, since any attack on inflation would hit at the privileges of specific interest groups, who threaten their fearsome counterattacks at the polls. But perhaps some politicians would be brave enough, and wise enough, to advocate steps that would earn the outrage of specific interests in the short run but gain the support of the inflation-strained majority over the longer haul. Among the steps that, taken together, could cut inflation:

Reduce the Budget. President Carter emptily claims that his budget for the next fiscal year is "tight," although it has soared since 1974 from less than $270 billion to more than $500 billion, and the planned deficit will run an inflationary $60 billion–plus for the second straight year. With the economy rising and unemployment falling, even Treasury Secretary W. Michael Blumenthal and the rest of Carter's closest economic advisers believe that the deficit should be contained. Wisconsin Democrat William Proxmire, one of the Senate's best economic thinkers, argues that the budget should be shrunk to $465 billion. At the very least, it could be reduced

[B]

to $480 billion by selective paring. If spending is brought down, the Government will be able to further cut personal and corporate taxes, which would offer the double benefit of strapping inflation and stimulating the economy. For invigorating the economy, lower taxes are more effective than higher Government spending.

Curb Regulation. The spreading powers of the Environmental Protection Agency, the Occupational Safety and Health Administration, the Equal Employment Opportunity Commission and hundreds of other regulatory agencies aggravate inflation by adding to the budget and, more important, swelling the costs of doing business. One significant step would be to hold down the EPA's "enforcement" spending, which is budgeted to jump from $73 million to almost $95 million. Every dollar devoted to EPA "enforcement" obliges U.S. business to invest many more dollars on nonproductive machinery, which then raises prices, reduces productive capital spending and retards hiring.

Restrain Social Security Benefits. They are scheduled to rise fast in the years ahead. By trimming the benefits, the nation can also pare the scheduled increases in Social Security payroll taxes.

Limit Federal Pay. The Government's workers commonly collect more salary and fringes than private workers in comparable jobs, and federal pay is budgeted to increase 6% in the next fiscal year. If Carter succeeded in cutting that back to 5% or less, he would both reduce inflation in the federal payroll and gain moral authority to advocate similar restraint in private wages.

Hold Down State Wages. Having urged a reduction in federal pay increases, the President then could ask states and localities to hold raises for their employees to 5% or less.

Cut Local Taxes. If their projected wage increases were reduced, the states and cities could trim their sales, income or property taxes. Another reason for reduction: many states and localities are enjoying budget surpluses.

Chop Farm Subsidies and Controls. Federal farm aid has grown fourfold in the past two years, to an estimated $7.9 billion, and the Senate passed a farm bill last month that will add $120 to $170 to the food bill of a family of four in the next fiscal year. As a counter to that expensive bill, President Carter last week recommended higher wheat subsidies and for the first time since the early 1970s offered corn and cotton subsidies to farmers who reduce plantings, which will surely raise food prices. There is no excuse for subsidies, despite some farmers' noisy threats of "strike." Farm prices have risen 13.9% since last September, and some food prices will shoot through the roof this spring because foul weather has badly hurt harvests of Soviet wheat and Brazilian soybeans.

Repeal Inflationary Special-Interest Laws. The Jones Act, which requires all goods moving between U.S. ports to travel aboard high-cost U.S. ships, has many inflationary consequences, including raising the price of Alaskan oil shipped to the West and Gulf Coasts. The Davis-Bacon Act, a relic of the Depression, swells construction costs by requiring, in effect, that union wages must be paid on all federally aided projects.

Hold Back the Minimum Wage. It jumped from $2.30 to $2.65 last January and is scheduled to rise to $2.90 next January and $3.35 in 1981. Besides being inflationary, the increases discourage hiring of the unskilled and the young.

Freeze Executive Pay. Federal Reserve Chief G. William Miller, who took a cut from $400,000 to $57,500 when he left the chairmanship of Textron, recommends that "top business executives demonstrate their leadership in the fight by holding down their own compensation." A one-year moratorium on raises by people earning, say, $100,000 or more would not make much economic difference, but it might be worth something symbolically.

The weak and perilous course would be to surrender to inflation on the presumption that interest groups are just too strong and the nation's will is too weak to fight it. In fact, President Carter has given in to many of the constituencies, firing up inflation by calling for large jumps in welfare and urban spending, in farm subsidies and tariffs on imports as varied as sugar, TV sets and, just last week, CB radios. So long as the Administration appears to have round heels, self-seeking groups—from coal miners to steelmakers—will continue to press their inflationary desires.

The President has said that when he returns from his overseas trip this week, he will produce a comprehensive anti-inflation plan. His economic advisers urge him to take a tough stand by calling for a reduction of subsidies, regulations and the growth of spending. Clearly, the immediate risks would be outweighed by the ultimate rewards. If the U.S. reduces domestic inflation, the dollar will rise, import prices will decline, purchasing power will expand, interest rates will fall, housing will climb, profits will increase, the stock market will turn up, capital spending will swell, more jobs will be created and business will flourish. In sum, the small sacrifices made by special groups will lead to big benefits for all.   — *Marshall Loeb*

QUESTIONS

(1) What explanation of the cause of inflation is being proposed here? Has this been the major factor in the U.S. inflation of the 1970's? What other factors have been important? Refer to passage A.

(2) Is this reasoning correct? If so, explain why. If not, explain why not. Refer to passage B.

(3) For each of the ten suggestions in the article outline which source of inflation it is suppose to cure and how.

Strength in Wages Despite High Unemployment

BY EDWIN L. DALE, JR.

WASHINGTON—Last year the nation had its highest unemployment in the 30 years since World War II, right? Right.

As a consequence of all this slack in the laobr force, the rate of wage increases slowed markedly, right? Wrong. As measured by the dominant corporate sector of the economy, total hourly compensation last year rose more than in any other year since World War II.

The Bureau of Labor Statistics reported last week that hourly compensation in nonfinancial corporations increased 10.2 percent last year, up from 1974's 9.6 percent [the previous record].

This, of course, seems to stand the basic principle of supply and demand on its head. The greater the excess supply of labor, the higher its price—how can that be?

The explanation does not lie to any great degree in the claim (offered by some on the basis of personal observations) that unemployment last year was not "really" very high—that vacancies could not be filled and the like.

The unemployment rate for prime workers, adult males, averaged 6.7 percent last year, more than double the rate for 1973 and almost double 1974. In six of the 12 months it was more than 7 percent. The rate for adult women averaged 8 percent for the year. So there was slack in the labor force by any test.

The fact is that there is no wholly convincing explanation for the extraordinary tendency of wages to rise regardless of labor market conditions. Here are some parts of the explanation:

§ In the unionized sector of the labor force (about one-fourth of the total and more than that in the corporate part) wages rose both because of previous contractual agreements and, in some cases, because of cost-of-living escalator clauses.

§ The wages of many non-union employes in establishments where the production force is unionized rise, by tradition in line with the union wages.

§ Although the new union contracts negotiated last year involved a relatively small number of workers, those that were negotiated continued to reflect union bargaining power and the impact of past inflation, not the state of unemployment in the economy. First-year wage and benefit increases averaged 11 percent. Even construction settlements were fairly large despite unemployment in that industry of close to 20 percent.

§ Perhaps because of habit or a sense of "fairness" or a desire to hang on to their experienced workers, employers appear resigned to paying annual wage increases, particularly when preceding inflation has clearly eroded real earnings.

§ Fairly liberal extended-unemployment compensation probably reduced the number of job seekers somewhat, thus weakening the link between the recorded unemployment rate, even for prime workers, and the excess supply of labor.

It is now fairly well established that preceding inflation is a major determinant of wage increases, almost regardless of the unemployment rate.

What are the implications of last year's puzzling experience?

Arthur F. Burns, chairman of the Federal Reserve Board, calls the trend of wage increases "disturbing." He noted in recent Congressional testimony that last year's average increases were "far above the long-term rate of growth in productivity," and he said that, "if wage settlements in major industries exceed those of 1975, a new explosion of wages, costs and prices may be touched off."

It is widely agreed that the increase in any year in "unit labor costs"—the excess of wage increases over productivity improvement—sets a kind of floor for the inflation rates. This showed up perfectly in last week's Bureau of Labor Statistics figures. Unit labor costs in the corporate sector rose 6.1 percent last year, which was just about the nation's underlying inflation rate for the year.

Charles L. Schultze of the Brookings Institution, identifying the underlying inflation rate with the rise in unit labor costs told a Congressional committee last week:

"After the first two post-war inflations, the underlying rate of inflation was significantly reduced by a short period of high unemployment. Since 1969, however, it appears that the effect of short spells of high unemployment in decelerating the underlying rate of inflation has been substantially weaker."

The basic phenomenon appears to be true almost regardless of what the Federal Reserve does with the money supply. If the Federal Reserve does not "validate" the higher prices resulting from higher labor costs by a sufficient increase in the money supply, the result is not less inflation but simply more layoffs.

Herbert Stein, of the University of Virginia, touched on this issue in Congressional testimony last week. Speaking of both fiscal and monetary policy, Mr. Stein said:

"With the Administration's policy the total demand for goods and services, in current dollars, would be rising by about 11 percent per annum [in 1976 and 1977]. The reason unemployment would be declining very slowly is that wage rates will be rising by 8 or 9 percent a year on the average.

"Whether there is a moral obligation to validate this rate of wage increase by pumping demand up sufficiently to reduce unemployment rapidly in the face of it, and whether it makes good sense to do so, are surely open question."

For the immediate future there is some reason to hope that the upward pressure of wages on prices will be moderated by the usual spurt in productivity that accompanies an economy recovering from recession. Over any sustained period, however, it is evident that the present inflation rate of about 6 percent cannot be cut much further as long as wages continue to rise at their current pace.

An inflation rate of 6 percent seems pleasant by comparison with what the nation experienced in 1973 and 1974. But it is far above what has been normal in this nation's history. It would cut the value of the dollar in half in about 12 years. It would forever bar a return to the moderate interest rates that were customary until about 1965.

The relation of wages to prices is not something newly discovered. In the happy days of the early 1960's, when consumer prices rose on the average less than 1.5 percent a year, wages rose on the average less than 4 percent a year.

Can anything be done? Dr. Burns and Mr. Schultze continue to place some faith and hope in "incomes policies"—by which they mean a non mandatory set of guidelines or other Government actions aimed at moderating the rate of wage increases. Dr. Burns is convinced that the nation will come around to such policies sooner or later, though he concedes that they have not worked well for any sustained period in other countries.

Britain now is very close to outright wage controls, and the experiment is succeeding. But no one knows how long it will continue to work.

Arthur M. Okun of the Brookings Institution was apparently the first to suggest an ingenious indirect way of curbing wages. This is to encourage the states, perhaps by Federal grants, to reduce or eliminate their sales taxes. This would directly reduce the price level (though only on a one-time basis) and correspondingly reduce the upward pressure on wages. Ideally, a kind of "virtuous circle" could set in, with slower wage increases leading in turn to less inflation.

Walter W. Heller of the University of Minnesota has suggested not only beginning to finance part of the cost of Social Security out of general revenues to prevent an increase in the payroll tax, but doing so in sufficient degree to permit an actual reduction in the tax. This would increase take-home pay and should reduce pressure for wage increases and, of course, it would also reduce employer costs. Where the "general revenues" are to come from is, of course, another question.

In any case, the nation now has clear-cut evidence that, if the aim is to slow wage inflation, deep recessions are not the way to achieve that goal.

(1) In light of the results in this article, do you think there is a stable trade-off in the short run between rates of inflation and unemployment? Why or why not?

(2) What do you think are the implications of this article for "cures" to the problem of "stag-flation"?

PUBLIC EMPLOYMENT

MILTON FRIEDMAN

It is by now widely recognized that there is no way to end inflation without a temporary slowdown in economic growth and a temporary increase in unemployment. In the search for measures to reduce these costs of stemming inflation, "public employment" has been receiving increasing attention. A typical proposal is that Congress appropriate in advance $4 billion to $5 billion or more a year to hire extra government employees, the program to be put into operation automatically when unemployment reaches a designated figure such as 5.5 or 6.0 per cent.

The program has great appeal. It appears to offer a way in which the government, while acting to halt inflation, can keep down the higher unemployment that is the most undesirable side effect of such action. But this appeal is spurious. It comes from looking only at the direct effects of the policy and neglecting its indirect effects. When both are taken into account, it turns out that "public employment" would increase, not decrease, the cost of stemming inflation.

The Seen and the Unseen

The neglect of indirect effects is a common source of economic fallacies. Let me illustrate by an example that is more transparent because by now we have had so much experience with it. In the past several decades we have been troubled by "urban blight." An appealing "solution" is to tear down the slums and rebuild them—whence came the massive "urban renewal" program. What happened? Slums were indeed torn down, which seemed all to the good, but in the process, housing occupied by lower-income groups was demolished and replaced by non-residential structures or by a smaller amount of middle- or upper-income housing. The total number of dwelling units was reduced, but the number of people requiring housing was not affected. Persons displaced by urban renewal had to look for housing elsewhere, which created slums where none had existed before. The program deserves the name it received of "Negro removal." It has added to "urban blight," not solved it.

"Public employment" suffers from precisely the same defect. It would in the first instance provide jobs for the unemployed, which seems all to the good. But where would the funds come from to pay their wages?

If the funds came from reducing other government expenditures, new government employees would simply replace other government employees with no gain in total employment and very likely a loss in efficiency.

If the funds came from imposing higher taxes, the taxpayers would have less to spend, which would reduce the number of persons they employ directly or indirectly. New government employees would simply replace persons employed in the private sector. "Make-work" would replace employment that met the private demands of taxpayers.

If the funds came from borrowing from the public, less credit would be available to lend to others. New government employees would simply replace persons employed in building houses or factories or machines that would have been financed by savings now absorbed by the public-employment program. Make-work would replace employment devoted to adding to our productive wealth.

The only other source of finance is printing or creating money. In this case, government demand would add to private demand and could create new jobs. But then it would be inflationary and so would undo with the left hand what the right hand was striving to achieve—namely, less inflation. The whole purpose is, after all, to reduce the rate at which total spending is increasing—for that is the way that inflation can be stemmed. If extra demand from "public employment" is desirable, then anti-inflation measures are being pushed too hard. It would be better simply to ease up on these measures than to offset one mistake with another.

The Right Approach

We have a responsibility to keep to a minimum the costs of ending inflation, and to assure that the disadvantaged do not bear a major part of those costs. The best way to minimize the withdrawal costs is by the widespread use of *escalator clauses.* The best way to protect the disadvantaged is by improving our system of welfare and of insurance against long-term unemployment. These measures are desirable for the long pull and not only for our present problem.

Throwing some people out of work in order to give jobs to others may have great political appeal. But it makes no economic sense.

QUESTIONS

(1) Explain why Friedman opposes bills to provide "public employment". See, for example, the second paragraph.

(2) Does the method used to finance the expenditures on public employment make any difference to Friedman? If so, how?

Why Inflation Persists

By Milton Friedman

Nearly three years ago, I wrote in this space: "Four times in the past fifteen years we have started on a cure for inflation. Three times we have abandoned the cure before it had time to complete its task—in 1963, 1967, 1971. Each time, the result has been a higher plateau of inflation, producing a new attempt at a cure. Will we make the same mistake the fourth time in 1975? Or this time, will we have the courage and the wisdom and the patience to see the cure through?" (NEWSWEEK, Nov. 4, 1974.)

ABANDONING THE CURE

As of today, the answer is that we have made the same mistake a fourth time. Once again, we have paid the cost of a recession to stem inflation, and, once again, we are in the process of throwing away the prize. From a high of more than 12 per cent in 1974 (from December 1973 to December 1974) inflation fell to less than 5 per cent (December 1975 to December 1976). It has now risen sharply, may temporarily recede as we work through the bulge produced by the special problem of the hard winter, but then, I fear, will resume its upward march, not to the "modest" 6 per cent the Administration is forecasting, but to at least several percentage points higher and possibly to double digits again by 1978 or 1979.

There is one and only one basic cause of inflation: too high a rate of growth in the quantity of money—too much money chasing the available supply of goods and services. These days, that cause is produced in Washington, proximately, by the Federal Reserve System, which determines what happens to the quantity of money; ultimately, by the political and other pressures impinging on the System, of which the most important are the pressures to create money in order to pay for exploding Federal spending and in order to promote the goal of "full employment." All other alleged causes of inflation—trade union intransigence, greedy business corporations, spendthrift consumers, bad crops, harsh winters, OPEC cartels and so on—are either consequences of inflation, or excuses by Washington, or sources of temporary blips of inflation.

There is one and only one basic cure for inflation: slowing monetary growth. But that cure is easier to state than to put into effect: witness our repeated abandonment of the cure. The Fed is supposedly independent. But, as Dooley said of the Supreme Court, "It follows the election returns." Its behavior reminds me of nothing so much as the remark attributed to a U.S. Army officer in Vietnam, "We destroyed the village in order to save it." Similarly, the Fed refrains from using its independence because it is afraid of losing it.

Listen to Chairman Arthur F. Burns in testimony to the House of Representatives (July 29, 1977):

"The trend of growth in monetary aggregates, I regret to say, is still too rapid. Even though the Federal Reserve has steadily sought during the past two years to achieve lower ranges for monetary expansion, the evolution of its projections has been extremely gradual; indeed, at the pace we have been moving [*note: with respect to projections, not behavior*] it would require perhaps a decade to reach rates of growth consistent with price stability. I must report, moreover, that despite the gradual reduction of projected growth ranges for the aggregates during the past two years, no meaningful reduction has as yet occurred in actual growth rates."

Meaning: promises have been in the right direction but too modest; performance has been in the wrong direction.

THE PERFORMANCE OF THE FED

The following table documents Chairman Burns's description of performance: the high rates of monetary growth from 1971 to early 1973 fostered the inflation that peaked in 1974. The sharply lower monetary-growth rates from 1973 to 1975 produced the serious recession of 1974-75 and the subsequent tapering off of inflation. The sharp rise in early 1975 sparked the recovery; the slowdown in late 1975 produced the economic pause in the second half of 1976 that played such a prominent role in the Ford-Carter election battle. Since then, monetary growth has been rising, not falling, and is now about back where it was in 1972.

Recent Rates of Monetary Growth
(per cent per year)

	M₁	M₂
December 1971 to January 1973	9.3	11.4
January 1973 to February 1975	4.5	7.7
February 1975 to June 1975	9.5	12.0
'une 1975 to December 1975	2.8	7.0
December 1975 to June 1976	5.8	10.5
June 1976 to August 1977	7.1	10.9

M₁ = currency plus adjusted demand deposits; M₂ = M₁ plus commercial bank time deposits other than large CD's

Inflation will not be stopped by words, only by actions. At the moment, we have the worst of two worlds. Nominal independence of the Federal Reserve without its effective exercise permits Congress and the President to evade responsibility for the creation of money to finance large government deficits. The power of Congress to legislate and of the President to approve such deficits without explicit responsibility for the resulting monetary growth gives the Federal Reserve an excuse for its inflationary behavior.

Again, let me quote Chairman Burns, this time from a speech on Aug. 13, 1977, proclaiming "The Importance of an Independent Central Bank":

"Theoretically, the Federal Reserve could thwart the non-monetary pressures that are tending to drive costs and prices higher by providing substantially less monetary growth than would be needed to accommodate these pressures fully. In practice, such a course would be fraught with major difficulty and considerable risk. Every time our government acts to enlarge the flow of benefits to one group or another the assumption is implicit that the means of financing will be available. A similar tacit assumption is embodied in every pricing decision, wage bargain, or escalator arrangement that is made by private parties or government. The fact that such actions may in combination be wholly incompatible with moderate monetary expansion is seldom considered by those who initiate them."

FISH OR CUT BAIT

It matters little whether the Federal Reserve is unable or unwilling to exercise its independence in deeds as well as words. In either case, let us be done with the fiction that "independence" is somehow or other a bastion against inflation. Let us put the responsibility for the rate of monetary growth—and therewith for the subsequent rate of inflation—squarely and openly on the Administration and Congress. Instead of simply requiring the Federal Reserve to *report* its "projections" or "targets" for monetary growth, let the Congress require the Fed to *achieve* specified rates of monetary growth (or specified levels of the quantity of money) within specified ranges of tolerance. That would combine responsibility and power. It would also enable the ordinary citizen to know whom to hold accountable for inflation.

(1) According to Friedman, "There is one and only one basic cause of inflation: too high a rate of growth in the quantity of money." Explain the assumptions behind this important monetarist conclusion.

(2) Friedman blames the Fed for the "stagflation" of the U.S. in the 1970s. What alternative explanations can you give for the inflation of 1973–74 and the recession of 1974–75?

(3) Consider the last paragraph. On what grounds would you disagree with Friedman's policy proposal concerning the money supply?

Steady As You Go

By Milton Friedman

The editors asked me to specify the economic policies that I would recommend to President-elect Carter *under present conditions*. I am the wrong person for that question. I oppose, and long have opposed, fine-tuning policies to every wiggle in the economic indicators. I favor, and long have favored, a policy of "steady as you go": a steady rate of monetary growth and a steady structure of taxes and government spending programs, with changes introduced solely to serve long-run objectives, not to lean against tomorrow's supposed wind. For money, long-run considerations call for a gradual reduction in the rate of monetary growth to a level consistent with zero inflation (about 0 to 2 per cent per year for M_1, 3 to 5 per cent for M_2). For taxes and spending, long-run considerations call for reducing both, relative to national income. That is the policy I favored a year ago, six months ago, and shall favor six months from now. Hence I am always in a difficult spot when asked, "What do you recommend *now*?"

Recent experience underscores the merits of that approach. Less than nine months ago, there was widespread euphoria: real output had risen in the first quarter of 1976 at the boom rate of 9.2 per cent per year. All was well. The economy was on the march. Three months ago, gloom overcame euphoria. The economy had slowed down. We were heading for renewed recession.

CHANGING WINDS

Only a little more than a month ago, President-elect Carter proclaimed that the economy was getting worse, that all his foreboding during the campaign was being realized. Today, glimmerings of euphoria have again begun to emerge. The latest tea leaves are more encouraging. Two months from now, for all we know, euphoria may again be in the ascendancy—that is about the time per-spective of Wall Street, Washington and the news media.

Suppose policy had been adjusted promptly to each change in the direction of the wind, and suppose—to strain the imagination even more—that that policy had been fully effective. At best, it takes some months for actions to have their effect. The actions taken to offset the spring breeze would have intensified the summer and autumn doldrums; the actions taken to offset those doldrums might turn a brisk spring 1977 breeze into a raging gale.

This sequence is not purely supposition. It is arguable that fine-tuning gyrations in monetary policy did intensify recent changes in economic growth. The money supply (defined as M_2, i.e., currency plus all commercial-bank deposits other than large CD's) grew at the annual rate of 11.8 per cent from February 1975 to July 1975, at 7.1 per cent from July 1975 to January 1976, at 10.6 per cent from January 1976 to July 1976, and has grown at 11.9 per cent since that period. I believe that these gyrations contributed to the initial rapid growth of output in 1976 and to the subsequent slowdown, and threaten to produce overheating of the economy in the coming months. Of course, the connection is far from precise. The astute reader will note that the changes in monetary growth preceded the subsequent changes in the economy by intervals that varied from a few months to nearly a year. That is a major reason why I oppose fine-tuning. We simply do not know enough—or, equivalently, the economy is too complex and variable—for us to be able to manipulate the fine-tuning dials with enough precision to get the desired results. We end up instead introducing additional disturbances to the economy.

GYRATING FED

Why the gyrations in monetary growth? Partly, because the Federal Reserve System was attempting to engage in fine-tuning; partly because the system has still not completely shed its schizophrenic attempt to control both interest rates and monetary growth; mostly, because the system continues to use obsolete and inefficient operating techniques to achieve its stated objective.

Finally, what about the implicit assumption of so much current talk that we know how to fine-tune; in particular, that a tax cut or an increase in government spending is "stimulative"? On that ground, a surtax was enacted in 1968 deliberately to stem inflation—and inflation accelerated. One example does not constitute a proof. But at least it may raise some question whether we are being offered penicillin or snake oil.

What Jimmy Should Do

By Paul A. Samuelson

President Carter's first task will be to ensure a vigorous recovery in 1977. Fortunately for us, he holds all the cards he needs.

His appointments have been well received—even by business, which is notoriously allergic to Democratic Presidents. Carter's victory has allayed the worst fears of consumers: since Election Day, Christmas-season buying and new-auto sales have risen on a seasonally corrected basis; helped by strike settlements, production and income have accelerated; even the stock market has regained its courage, feasting on a diet of low interest rates and daydreaming of a Carter honeymoon ahead. The phlegmatic computers of the consensus forecasters no longer flash the red lights of a recession to arrive by late 1977.

MACROECONOMIC IMPERATIVES

Carter's stars are favorable. But he must make his own luck. To achieve the 6 per cent real rate of growth agreed upon as a reasonable target by President-elect Carter and Fed chairman Arthur Burns, three determined programs

must be pushed in early 1977.

1. *There must be a tax cut of $10 billion to $20 billion.* (I have just resurveyed the evidence on tax-change potency in 1964, 1968, 1975, and in half a dozen other relevant incidents here and abroad. Conclusions: any tax cut politically feasible early this year will in fact add to needed growth in output, employment, real income, profits and wages.)

2. Nixon and Ford have left the nation with an accrued deficit of vital public-sector needs, local and Federal. Tearing up Ford's lame-duck budget, *President Carter and Congress should expand the total of fiscal spending stimulus in 1977.*

This recommendation is squarely compatible with Carter's pledge to cut out waste and inefficiency in government spending. By all means, kill the boondoggle of a B-1 manned-bomber program. Consolidate agencies. Review old programs to redline and terminate the failures.

But reinstate a Federal establishment responsive to human needs at every level, local as well as national. Make good

on those promises of private-sector and public-sector jobs programs. The nation will need them no less in prosperous than in recession times. Get on with the overdue task of more equitably sharing the burdens of the big cities.

3. Congress and the President, to say nothing of the American people, expect something more of the Federal Reserve than paranoid sermonizing on the perils of inflation. Any fool banker can sing that song in season and out. What the nation hopes for in Governor Burns and his colleagues is discrimination between price inflation induced by an overemployed and overheated economy and that induced by OPEC juntas or worldwide crop shortages.

Eschewing belligerence and ignoring the advice of extremists, President Carter, Senator Proxmire, Representative Reuss and the Congressional leadership can work with the Federal Reserve to *ensure monetary growth and credit availability compatible with bringing the unemployment rate down in the next two years from its recent 8.1 per cent level to below 6 per cent. After that is done,* a bipartisan Federal Reserve Board can come into the court of public debate with clean hands: its counsel in the search for the golden mean between accelerating inflation and mass unem-

ployment will then be accorded the attention that the board has earned.

Close elections make for good policy. Lively debate subjects each proposal to audit. The cocksure dogmas of laissez faire and centralism lose out in the competitive marketplace of ideas.

MICROECONOMIC OPPORTUNITIES

With a bit of good fortune, Carter's stock may have risen much by a year from now. What good is it for a humanitarian to work up a line of credit with the people if he does not have plans to spend it in good causes?

There are plenty of inefficiencies in our mixed economy that no conservative can succeed in reforming. A Franklin Roosevelt, Kennedy, or Carter, having demonstrated his bona fides with the middle- and lower-income classes, could hope to make some progress with the energy mess, the regulatory snafus, the logjams of health care, and the replacement of the present complicated state and local welfare structures by a comprehensive negative income tax.

But first Jimmy Carter must earn his spurs. To do that, as John F. Kennedy learned in the 1960s, he must resist trying to curry favor with the conservative financiers and business executives whose advice has already served Gerald Ford and the nation badly. Besides—Kennedy also learned—that ploy to curry favor won't work anyway.

These Nobel Laureates have offered substantially different prescriptions for our economic recovery from recessions. Explain how these prescriptions stem directly from the "Keynesian" vs. "Monetarist" view of how the aggregate economy works.

Part III

MICROECONOMIC PRINCIPLES IN ACTION

Airline takes the marginal route

Continental Air Lines, Inc., last year filled only half the available seats on its Boeing 707 jet flights, a record some 15 percentage points worse than the national average.

By eliminating just a few runs—less than 5%—Continental could have raised its average load considerably. Some of its flights frequently carry as few as 30 passengers on the 120-seat plane. But the improved load factor would have meant reduced profits.

For Continental bolsters its corporate profits by deliberately running extra flights that aren't expected to do more than return their out-of-pocket costs—plus a little profit. Such marginal flights are an integral part of the over-all operating philosophy that has brought small, Denver-based Continental—tenth among the 11 trunk carriers—through the bumpy postwar period with only one loss year [**BW** Sep.23'61.p90].

Chief contribution. This philosophy leans heavily on marginal analysis. And the line leans heavily on Chris F. Whelan (picture),* vice-president in charge of economic planning, to translate marginalism into hard, dollars-and-cents decisions (box, page 56).

Getting management to accept and apply the marginal concept probably is the chief contribution any economist can make to his company. Put most simply, marginalists maintain that a company should undertake any activity that adds more to revenues than it does to costs—and not limit itself to those activities whose returns equal average or "fully allocated" costs.

The approach, of course, can be applied to virtually any business, not just to air transportation. It can be used in consumer finance, for instance, where the question may be whether to make more loans—including more bad loans—if this will increase net profit. Similarly, in advertising, the decision may rest on how much extra business a dollar's worth of additional advertising will bring in, rather than pegging the advertising budget to a percentage of sales—and, in insurance, where setting high interest rates to discourage policy loans may actually damage profits by causing policyholders to borrow elsewhere.

Communication. Whelan finds all such cases wholly analogous to his run of problems, where he seeks to keep his company's eye trained on the big objective: net profit.

He is a genially gruff, shirt-sleeves kind of airline veteran, who resembles more a sales-manager type than an economist. This facet of his personality helps him "sell" ideas internally that might otherwise be brushed off as merely theoretical or too abstruse.

Last summer, Whelan politely chewed out a group of operational researchers at an international conference in Rome for being incomprehensible. "You have failed to educate the users of your talents to the potential you offer," he said. "Your studies, analyses, and reports are couched in tables that sales, operations, and maintenance personnel cannot comprehend."

Full-time job. Whelan's work is a concrete example of the truth in a crack by Prof. Sidney Alexander of MIT—formerly economist for Columbia Broadcasting System—that the economist who understands marginal analysis has a "full-time job in undoing the work of the accountant." This is so, Alexander holds, because the practices of accountants —and of most businesses—are permeated with cost allocation directed at average, rather than marginal, costs.

In any complex business, there's likely to be a big difference between the costs of each company activity as it's carried on the accounting books and the marginal or "true" costs that can determine whether or not the activity should be undertaken.

The difficulty comes in applying the simple "textbook" marginal concept to specific decisions. If the economist is unwilling to make some bold simplifications, the job of determining "true" marginal costs may be highly complex, time-wasting, and too expensive. But even a rough application of marginal principles may come closer to the right answer for business decision-makers than an analysis based on precise average-cost data.

Proving that this is so demands economists who can break the crust of corporate habits and show concretely why the typical manager's

response—that nobody ever made a profit without meeting all costs—is misleading and can reduce profits. To be sure, the whole business cannot make a profit unless average costs are met; but covering average costs should not determine whether any particular activity should be undertaken. For this would unduly restrict corporate decisions and cause managements to forgo opportunities for extra gains.

Approach. Management overhead at Continental is pared to the bone, so Whelan often is thrown such diverse problems as soothing a ruffled city council or planning the specifications for the plane the line will want to fly in 1970. But the biggest slice of his time goes to schedule planning—and it is here that the marginal concept comes most sharply into focus.

Whelan's approach is this: He considers that the bulk of his scheduled flights have to return at least their fully allocated costs. Overhead, depreciation, insurance are very real expenses and must be covered. The out-of-pocket approach comes into play, says Whelan, only after the line's basic schedule has been set.

"Then you go a step farther," he says, and see if adding more flights will contribute to the corporate net. Similarly, if he's thinking of dropping a flight with a disappointing record, he puts it under the marginal microscope: "If your revenues are going to be more than your out-of-pocket costs, you should keep the flight on."

By "out-of-pocket costs" Whelan means just that: the actual dollars that Continental has to pay out to run a flight. He gets the figure not by applying hypothetical equations but by circulating a proposed schedule to every operating department concerned and finding out just what extra expenses it will entail. If a ground crew already on duty can service the plane, the flight isn't charged a penny of their salary expense. There may even be some costs eliminated in running the flight; they won't need men to roll the plane to a hangar, for instance, if it flies on to another stop.

Most of these extra flights, of course, are run at off-beat hours, mainly late at night. At times,

Reproduced from *Business Week,* April 20, 1963, pp. 111-112, 114 by special permission. All rights are reserved. Copyright 1963 by McGraw-Hill, Inc. Questions have been taken from G. Leland Bach, *ECONOMICS,* 9th Edition, Englewood Cliffs, N.J.: Prentice-Hall, Inc. 1978.

though, Continental discovers that the hours aren't so unpopular after all. A pair of night coach flights on the Houston-San Antonio-El Paso-Phoenix-Los Angeles leg, added on a marginal basis, have turned out to be so successful that they are now more than covering fully allocated costs.

Alternative. Whelan uses an alternative cost analysis closely allied with the marginal concept in drawing up schedules. For instance, on his 11:11 p.m. flight from Colorado Springs to Denver and a 5:20 a.m. flight the other way, Continental uses Viscounts that, though they carry some cargo, often go without a single passenger. But the net cost of these flights is less than would be the rent for overnight hangar space for the Viscount at Colorado Springs.

And there's more than one absolute-loss flight scheduled solely to bring passengers to a connecting Continental long-haul flight; even when the loss on the feeder service is considered a cost on the long-haul service, the line makes a net profit on the trip.

Continental's data handling system produces weekly reports on each flight, with revenues measured against both out-of-pocket and fully allocated costs. Whelan uses these to give each flight a careful analysis at least once a quarter. But those added on a marginal basis get the fine-tooth-comb treatment monthly.

The business on these flights tends to be useful as a leading indicator, Whelan finds, since the off-peak traffic is more than normally sensitive to economic trends and will fall off sooner than that on the popular-hour flights. When he sees the night coach flights turning in consistently poor showings, it's a clue to lower his projections for the rest of the schedule.

Unorthodox. There are times, though, when the decisions dictated by the most expert marginal analysis seem silly at best, and downright costly at worst. For example, Continental will have two planes converging at the same time on Municipal Airport in Kansas City, when the new schedules take effect.

This is expensive because, normally, Continental doesn't have the facilities in K.C. to service two planes at once; the line will have to lease an extra fuel truck and hire three new hands—at a total monthly cost of $1,800.

But, when Whelan started pushing around proposed departure times in other cities to avoid the double landing, it began to look as though passengers switching to competitive flights leaving at choicer hours, would lose Continental $10,000 worth of business each month. The two flights will be on the ground in K.C. at the same time.

Full work week. This kind of scheduling takes some 35% of Whelan's time. The rest of his average work week breaks down this way: 25% for developing near-term, point-to-point traffic forecasts on which schedules are based; 20% in analyzing rates—Whelan expects to turn into a quasi-lawyer to plead Continental's viewpoint before the Civil Aeronautics Board; 20% on long-range forecasts and the where-should-we-go kind of planning that determines both which routes the line goes after and which it tries to shed. (Whelan's odd jobs in promotion, public relations, and general management don't fit into that time allotment; he says they "get stuck on around the side.")

The same recent week he was working on the data for his Kansas City double-landing problem, for instance, he was completing projections for the rest of 1963 so that other departments could use them for budget making, and was scrutinizing actions by Trans World Airlines, Inc., and Braniff Airways, Inc. TWA had asked CAB approval for special excursion fares from Eastern cities to Pacific Coast terminals; Whelan decided the plan worked out much the same as the economy fare on Continental's three-class service, so will neither oppose nor match the excursion deal. Braniff had just doubled its order—to 12—for British Aircraft Corp.'s 111 jets. Whelan was trying to figure out where they were likely to use the small planes, and what effect they would have on Continental's share of competing routes in Texas and Oklahoma.

At the same time, Whelan was meeting with officials of Frontier Airlines and Trans-Texas, coordinating the CAB-ordered takeover by the feeder lines of 14 stops Continental is now serving with leased DC-3s.

And he was struggling, too, with a knotty problem in consumer economics: He was trying to sell his home on Denver's Cherry Vale Drive and buy one in Los Angeles, where Continental will move its headquarters this summer.

QUESTIONS

Is Continental Airlines right in using marginal analysis to decide whether to add flights? What if each flight, looked at individually, more than covers marginal cost, but added together they don't cover the firm's total costs? Would this latter case invalidate the marginal principle?

Commodities

Mink Farming Is Growing More Scarce As Costs Rise and Fur Demand Declines

By Michael L. Geczi
Staff Reporter of The Wall Street Journal

NEW YORK—Mink farms could well be on the endangered-species list.

The animals themselves never have reached an endangered status, but the number of U.S. farms raising the small mammals for their pelts has decreased sharply in recent years. In the industry's peak year, 1966, about 6,000 mink farms were operating in the U.S. Today, there are 1,221 according to the U.S. Agriculture Department.

Despite slight increases the past two years, total pelt production last year was 3.1 million, or half of the record 6.2 million pelts produced in 1966. Annual sales at the auction level, where most pelts are sold, were about $54 million in 1974, according to one estimate, down from more than $120 million in the mid-1960s.

The smaller operations have been the hardest hit. "The mom and pop outfits and the part-timers were the ones that folded," says an Agriculture Department official. "The bigger farms have kept operating."

Some industry officials say a profitable mink farm of any size is rare. "We've been in dire straits for the past four or five years," says Robert Langenfeld, president of Associated Fur Farms Inc., New Holstein, Wis., one of the nation's largest mink farms.

[A]

The industry's descent has been as rapid as its rise in the 1950s and 1960s, during which time mink grew in popularity as a fashionable status symbol. Growth was aided by the development of new colors (there are currently 13). As producers' feed and labor costs remained relatively stable in the face of strong demand, more people entered the industry.

Unsold Inventories

Growth proved to be too rapid, however; large unsold inventories from the record 1966 crop caused a price bust in 1967, and

[B]

the situation has worsened since. Feed and labor costs have climbed rapidly. Competition from less-expensive foreign pelts has heightened.

Perhaps most important, mink has lost much of its prestige. Industry officials say the desire to wear a mink coat has in many instances given way to ecological concerns.

Cries from conservationists "caused a mass reaction for the 'poor animal,'" says Louis Henry, president of Hudson Bay Fur Sales Inc., The Hudson's Bay Co. unit that handles about two-thirds of the pelts sold at auction in the U.S. annually.

Mr. Henry recalls that in 1966 pelts sold at auction for an average of $24 each. The going price today for a mutation (colored) skin is about $14. Dark furs bring a slightly higher price.

[C]

In the 1960s, a mink producer would net about $5 on a mutation pelt, says Mr. Langenfeld. "Now," he says, "we're losing about $3 a pelt on our mutations." He says it costs the company $17 to raise a kit, or young mink, and bring its pelt to auction.

Mink farmers breed their animals in March. The kits—usually four to a litter—are born in early May. They're raised for six months before being killed—humanely, producers say—by gas or electrocution. The skins then are removed and readied for sale.

Finicky Animal

In most cases they are sent to one of four main U.S. auction centers, in New York City, Seattle, Minneapolis and Milwaukee. Fees received by one of the two associations that offer the pelts for sale and by the company conducting the auction can take up to 7.75% of the pelt's selling price.

The price the producers get for their pelts is their reward for raising a finicky animal that prefers only the freshest meat, poultry and fish. Most mink farms have expensive refrigeration, grinding and mixing machines, and also must hire extra help to thaw and feed daily rations to the animals. All this causes the mink's diet to represent more than half of the total cost of raising a mink to pelt-producing size.

Mink researchers have been working to develop a dry diet that would be more economical and still satisfy the taste and nutritional requirements of the animal. Some farmers are using the dry diets, but they are far from gaining industry-wide acceptance.

U.S. producers are said to produce a high-quality pelt much prized by those who don't mind paying handsomely for a coat or stole. But about half of the six million or so pelts used annually in the U.S. are less-expensive foreign ones produced mainly in Scandinavia. Some industry officials say an increasing number of garments made from these pelts are being sold to people who formerly would have bought the more expensive item made from U.S.-produced pelts.

Mr. Henry says the worst may be over, however. "I think it (sales) will stabilize just about where it is," he says. Some observers expect a pickup in business as the recession eases.

Will business ever return to the good old days? "I don't know any mink farmers who ever had any good old days," says Mr. Langenfeld.

EXERCISES AND QUESTIONS

(1) Regarding passage A: Illustrate (graphically) the effect of the increased demand on price, output, profit in the short run and long run, both for the individual firm and the industry.

(2) Starting with your graphs at the conclusion of question 1, show the effect of each of the following:

(a) "Mink has lost most of its prestige."
(b) "Feed and labor costs have climbed rapidly."
(c) The results at the beginning of the article indicate that industry output has declined and the number of firms has fallen. Is this result dependent on the relative sizes of the effects above? (or does the result indicated at the beginning of the article follow automatically from the nature of the shifts in the curves?)

(3) Regarding passage C: Has the industry reached a new long-run competitive equilibrium? Show on a diagram (or explain intuitively) why a mink producer might continue to produce even if this person observed that "We're losing about $3 a pelt on our mutations."

CALIFORNIA:

Sour Grapes

This ought to be a time of rejoicing in the vineyards of California. The crop of wine grapes has rarely been richer, the harvest is nearly complete—and Americans are drinking more California wine than ever before. But not quite enough, as it turns out. Because of overplanting during the past five years of unprecedented boom, the grape crop this year is simply too big to squeeze. As a result, a number of growers were licking their financial wounds last week—while wine lovers were licking their chops in anticipation of what one expert predicts will be five years of top-quality California wine offered at bargain-basement prices.

The cycle started back in the early 1970s when Americans suddenly turned to wine, particularly moderate-priced brands from California. Sales began to skyrocket—and wholesale grape prices began to rise as well. Cabernet Sauvignon grapes, California's finest black variety, climbed to a peak of $810 a ton in 1973. The Bank of America confidently predicted that the decade would bring "the strongest growth in wine markets ever recorded." Industrial conglomerates began buying vineyards, and so did hastily organized partnerships of airline pilots, doctors, lawyers and other professional people with money to invest. Since it takes at least three years to bring a vineyard to maturity, the new growers began planting as fast as they could. In 1969, there were 450,000 acres of grapes in California; this year, there are 650,000.

The cork finally popped. Even though the sale of California wine will increase by 9 per cent this year, that is not enough to soak up the added production—and prices for grapes and wine alike are tumbling. Chardonnay grapes, for example, went for $815 a ton two years ago; they are now selling for from $350 to $400. The result is a number of bankrupt vineyards and a slash in winery profits. Prudential Insurance Co. of America recently foreclosed on 2,000 acres of wine grapes in the Fresno area, and Roger Hoag, a company official, predicts it will be three years before many investors have any hope of getting back in the black. "There will be a lot of vineyards pulled out," Hoag said. "This is the only way the overplanting can be rectified."

The lingering effects of the recession are a major factor in the crisis in the vineyards. When they buy wine, Americans now tend to prefer lower-priced brands—partly because of price and partly because they have become more sophisticated in their tastes, realizing that the best wine is not always the more expensive one. "In the past twelve months, the consumer has been going for attractive price-value relationships," notes George Vare Jr. of Geyser Peak Winery. "Wines over $3 a bottle are not getting near the play they were before the housewife got hit by the crunch." As a result, grapes that once went only into higher-priced premium wines are now being used to produce jugs of good reds and whites at bargain prices. Italian Swiss Colony recently introduced a Cabernet Sauvignon, once the most costly red wine, at only $1.59 a bottle. Experts label it the best California wine buy on the market.

Blessing: The shake-out in the grape-and-wine industry will be a mixed blessing, according to many in the industry. Over the next five years, says Robert Mondavi, head of Robert Mondavi Winery in Oakville, Calif., some of the marginal operators in the business will be hurt—but the public won't. Not only will growers be forced to unload their big inventories at lower prices, but new techniques promise higher-quality wine than ever before. The next five years, Mondavi promises, should be no less than a golden age for oenophiles—and in the long run, for the vintners as well.

—TOM NICHOLSON with WILLIAM J. COOK in San Francisco

QUESTIONS

(1) Making explicit reference to the cost curves of the firms and the industry (which you should put on a well-labeled graph), explain why the price of grapes rose and then fell.

(a) Did the price fall because the demand curve shifted to the left?

(b) Is the price fall evidence of "overplanting," that is, does it indicate that production should not have taken place?

(2) The article states that some vineyards are "bankrupt". Does this mean they should stop producing grapes? Will they stop producing grapes?

(3) Should the government have intervened either to prevent the price rise or the price fall? Why or why not?

Dark Days for Scotland's Own

Taxes and America's desertion to vodka pour gloom upon the distillers of Scotch.

By PETER T. KILBORN

DUMGOYNE, Scotland—It seems quiet enough at the rural, picturesque Glengoyne distillery here to hear the worts fermenting into the wash that eventually becomes a few drops in the barrel of the most successful export that Scotland has ever produced, Scotch whisky.

It is, in fact, uncommonly quiet.

Glengoyne, the source of one of the elite, single-malt whiskies that are blended with more plebian corn-derived grain whiskies in the secret recipe of the Cutty Sark brand, is working only five days a week, rather than the usual seven. The same is true at many of the 129 distilleries in Scotland.

Scotch whisky has just come out of the worst year in memory, and the industry doubts that 1976 will be much better.

Scotland's distillers, blenders and bottlers produced 152 million gallons of whisky last year, down more than 17 percent from the 1974 level.

For the industry, accustomed to 8 and 10 per cent annual increases, said Alan Gray, a whisky industry expert at the Glasgow stock brokerage firm of Campbell, Neill & Company, "there has never been a decline like that."

Here at Glengoyne, 14 miles north of Glasgow, Scotch is made as it always has been. Starting with partially germinated barley, 12 men guide the product through pipes, hoppers, huge pine fermenting vats, and 40-foot-tall copper stills into oak casks where it is aged at least five years before being used in the company's own brands or sold to other distillers.

One of the industry's basic complaints is strikingly evident here. The distillery provides two homes on its grounds, one for the manager and one, at a modest rent, to the Government's tax man. He's here to make sure that not a drop of Glengoyne malt whisky leaves here without his knowing it.

Americans are a part of the industry's overall problem. The world's leading consumers of Scotch, importing half of all that Britain sells abroad, Americans have been switching to vodka. Vodka sales now exceed not only those of Scotch in the United States market, but also of home-grown bourbon.

Last year, Americans bought 7.8 percent less Scotch than they did in 1974. Much of what they did buy was not the well-known, bottled-in-Scotland brands such as Cutty Sark, Johnnie Walker and J&B, but humbler concoctions with nobler names, such as King George IV and Vat Gold, that are shipped in bulk as concentrates to be diluted and bottled in the United States.

Business was bad in Britain, too. Consumers, pinched by falling living standards, have been cutting back on everything from beer to champagne. Scotch sales fell 6 percent in volume and the industry thinks it will be another year before domestic sales revive.

A lot of the problem is price, and a lot of the price is taxes. A fifth of Johnnie Walker Red Label sells at retail in Britain today for the equivalent of about $7. Of that, about $5.60, including $1.28 that was added last year alone, goes to the Government. Earlier this month the take went even higher; Denis Healey, Chancellor of the Exchequer, announced another 60-cent tax hike on fifths of hard liquor in his annual budget message.

Heavy taxation in Britain, industry executives think,

helps set the pattern that **tax** authorities in other countries follow.

"In the last year, 38 countries put various new impositions of some form or another on whisky," said John A. R. MacPhail, managing director of Robertson and Baxter, the Scotch whisky blender that owns the Glengoyne distillery. In Brazil, he said, a fifth of Cutty Sark costs the equivalent of $34.

Scotch, like other liquor, has always been a vulnerable target for taxes. "It's a luxury item," Mr. McPhail said, "and people like it."

But there's a newer, accelerating trend to use the tax system to do what prohibition laws have failed to do—curtail alcoholism. Early this year, a prominent Glasgow health official disclosed that alcoholism in northern Scotland, the center of the industry, was 12 times as serious as in England, and that it was a major cause of serious crime.

Meanwhile, during the last gasps of Wall Street's go-go era a few years ago, scotch whisky became a problem of another sort, as an "investment vehicle."

Little-known futures brokers offered speculators investments in whisky that was maturing in the distilleries' casks. In five or six years it would age to liquid gold, it was hoped, and would then be sold to bottlers for blending.

Most investors bought grain whisky, distilled in Scotland from American corn and used as the tasteless base of blended whiskies. Wiser, or more fortunate, investors bought single-malt whiskies, such as the one produced here, that are made from Scottish barley.

Grain whiskies bought four years ago for about $3 a gallon are now worth about $1, according to industry sources, because of oversupply. Some of the higher grade malts, on the other hand, have at least maintained their original values.

A few investors are almost entirely out of pocket—those who bought blends. Bottlers do their own blending, so most of the speculators' holdings are worthless.

"A blend," said a leading Scottish broker who was not involved in the futures activity, "is like a sausage. You approach it with fear in case it's trying to hide something."

Most of the futures brokers have now disappeared, creating a problem for the Scotch Whisky Association in London which never included them among its members.

"We get letters every week from Americans saying 'we have this' and 'we have that' and can we help them?" said Richard Grindall, general secretary of the association. He refers them to leading brokers, but promises nothing.

There are other problems for the industry. The price of barley, the grain on which all Scotch malt whisky is built, jumped 40 percent last year because of grain shortages elsewhere, and while that price has begun to recede, the recession that deflated the American market last year is still running hard in Britain.

Nearly 85 percent of all the Scotch produced is sold abroad and because of an unaccountable surge in demand from Japan, exports actually rose last year, although by an uncharacteristically low 3 percent. Scotch accounts for 25 percent of all Scottish exports and about 2 percent of British exports.

The industry is dominated by a single concern, the Distillers Company, purveyors of such brands as Johnnie Walker, Dewar's, White Horse and Haig, as well as most of the whisky shipped in bulk. Last year the company is believed to have amassed slightly more than half the industry's total sales of about $900 million.

More characteristic of the Scotch-producing world, however, is the jerrybuilt assemblage of companies involved with the Glengoyne Distillery. It is owned by Lang Brothers, which in turn is owned by Robertson and Baxter. Robertson and Baxter also owns a cooperage that makes oak casks to age Glengoyne's whisky; it sells the brands of a company that owns other distilleries, and it owns half the Glasgow company where Cutty Sark and several other brands are blended and bottled.

Robertson and Baxter, like many in the industry, is privately owned and discloses nothing about its earnings or even its sales.

Its principal owners are three unmarried sisters, all over 60—Ethel, Agnes, and Elspreth Robertson, granddaughters of the founder.

EXERCISE AND QUESTIONS

(1) Illustrate, for the firm, and industry, the effect of each of the following on output and price:

(a) Demand for scotch declines as Americans switch to Vodka.

(b) Sales taxes are imposed by both the U.S. and British governments.

(c) Price of grain is increased.

(2) What has been the net effect on price? Output? (Can you tell from the qualitative change or do you need to compare the relative magnitudes?)

Lag in Tanker Business Puts the Squeeze On Builders and Owners—as Well as Banks

By JOHN D. WILLIAMS
Staff Reporter of THE WALL STREET JOURNAL

Cloverton Shipping Co., a Liberian-registered concern owned by U.S. interests, recently canceled orders with a Swedish shipbuilder for two 360,000-ton oil tankers. The reason; inability to line up charter customers for 1977.

In West Germany, a major bank recently foreclosed on a 109,000-ton, seven-year-old tanker, taking it from its Norwegian operator and selling it to a Greek concern. The new owner was granted a two-year moratorium on principal payments under the new mortgage.

And m Oslo, Hilmar Reksten, a major shipowner, defaulted on orders for a total of six big tankers that were to be built there by the Aker Group. An arbitration panel recently awarded Aker the equivalent of about $67 million in cancellation payments for four of the ships. Mr. Reksten has been severely hurt by low tanker rates and soaring operating costs.

As these examples suggest, the oil-tanker business isn't exactly booming. Overcapacity troubles had been predicted by experts as long ago as 1970, but it took the Mideast oil boycott, the quadrupling of oil prices since October 1973 and international economic woes to bring it all to a head.

Tanker Orders Canceled

Of the world-wide fleet of 4,000 tankers, 433 are laid up in port with no business—a record number. In the Persian Gulf, some 20 ships are riding at anchor, waiting for cargo that may or may not materialize. Many of the tankers that do have oil to carry are poking along at slower than normal speeds to save fuel. All told, shipowners have canceled orders for 100 tankers since last November.

[A]

Most observers figure that order cancellations and increased scrappings by shipowners will eventually bring things back into line, probably within three years. But in the meantime, everyone agrees it's going to be tough sailing for shipbuilders and owners, as well as for the array of international banks that have lent money to the industry.

Warns J. A. Waage, an executive vice president of New York's Manufacturers Hanover Trust Co., "The (tanker) situation is one of the biggest clouds on the horizon of international banking."

That certainly wasn't the case in 1973, when there was an unprecedented demand for tankers to haul oil to the U.S., Europe and Japan, where industrial production was running high. Charter rates were at record highs, with some independent owners grossing as much as $10 million on a single voyage. With those kinds of figures at stake, bankers were more than eager to lend money for new ships. And a record 105 million tons of tankers—equal to over 1,000 tankers of average size—were ordered that year. That was double the previous record in 1972.

But following the Mideast oil boycott, oil consumption in the U.S., Western Europe and Japan fell by about 5% in 1974, after growing at a 10% rate in 1973. The world skidded from boom to recession. And the world-wide tanker-fleet capacity rose by about 18% in 1974. (The lead time for a big tanker is about two years, and previously ordered ships are still being turned out at the rate of six a week.)

Some banks have had to make loan concessions to their shipbuilder clients. Last month, for example, Chase Manhattan Bank agreed to substitute a six-year, $65 million term loan to Seatrain Lines Inc. of New York without any payment of principal in the first two years. It replaced a $65 million short-term loan that has been overdue since early 1973. Seatrain builds tankers for others and also operates its own oil tankers and ocean freighters.

A Not-So-Halcyon Tanker

Bankers Trust Co., New York, holds a $19.5 million second mortgage on one of the world's most famous tankers, the 226,700-ton Halcyon the Great, sold at a court auction recently in London to a Hong Kong shipping man. The tanker had previously been owned by a diversified British travel company that went bankrupt last August. And in a well-publicized sea chase, the Royal Canadian Mounted Police tried in vain to slap a creditor's lien on the ship last October while it was trying to escape Canadian waters.

Overall estimates of international banks' outstanding loans to the industry are difficult to obtain, and most major U.S. and London bankers flatly refuse to discuss the matter. But one European banking source notes that many oil-tanker loans are secured through government credits or similar governmental help. He estimates that at most, possibly a half-dozen European banks, all of them secondary lending institutions, are overcommitted in tanker loans. Some, he concedes, could sink as a result of an unsecured loan to a foundering tanker man. But so far that hasn't happened.

Neither have any shipyards closed down, though one New York banking official predicts that "tanker assembly lines will grind to a halt by the second quarter of next year." The big Japanese shipyards, such as the Nagasaki facility of Mitsubishi Heavy Industries Ltd., produce about half the world's oil tankers. But spokesmen for the Japanese concerns decline to discuss the situation.

One large U.S. shipbuilder that has been affected is Todd Shipyards Corp., New York, which had a loss of $43.4 million in the fiscal year ended March 31. The company has halted a planned expansion of its Los Angeles yard because orders for eight 90,000-ton tankers were canceled. (The orders were canceled largely at Todd's request because they were on a fixed-price basis and Todd's costs were soaring.)

Unprofitable Rates

[B]

Many owners are chartering out their tankers at rates far lower than what they need to cover operating expenses—just to keep their crews intact or simply to get their ships home for lay-up. Exxon Corp. reportedly just chartered for $900,000 a year a Japanese tanker that costs $2 million a year to operate. One reason for the seemingly illogical deal: Japanese union rules require the owner to pay its seagoing crew its full wages whether or not the ship is employed.

[C]

Meanwhile, scrapping of old tankers is easing some of the pressure on the market.

In the first five months of this year 135 tankers totaling 3.6 million tons were scrapped, well above the 1.9 million tons scrapped in all of 1974. Scrap concerns in Taiwan and India pay $95 to $98 a ton for scrap metal. And some ship brokers say buyers currently have a chance to make a profitable two-way play on a tanker purchase: for chartering if the market improves or for scrapping if it doesn't.

Indeed, there are plenty of tanker bargains around. Arne Naess & Co. Inc., a New York ship broker, says prices today are about 10% of what they were at the peak in June 1973. Brokers report that the Liberian-registered Benjamin Coates, a 50,000-ton tanker built in 1960 was recently sold for $1.1 million, only slightly above what its scrap value would be.

QUESTIONS AND EXERCISES

(1) Draw the industry demand and supply curves for oil tanker services now and three years from now. Draw the corresponding cost and revenue picture for a typical tanker operator now and three years from now. See passage A.

(2) Consider section B. Explain why the Japanese shipowner was profit-maximizing even though he took losses.

(3) Consider section C. Since the oil tanker has positive scrap value, does this affect the supply curve for tanker services?

Commodities

Bauxite-Producing Nations' Price Push Eases Some in Wake of Aluminum Slump

By Gay Sands Miller

Staff Reporter of **The Wall Street Journal**

Cracks are appearing in the cartel-like campaign by some bauxite-producing nations to get more money for ore mined in their countries.

As a result, North American aluminum companies, which use bauxite to make aluminum, are growing less nervous about their bauxite supplies. "We don't expect rapid increases in bauxite prices" in the foreseeable future, says one major U.S. producer.

Such talk hardly resembles the tense mood of 1974, when Jamaica led six producers' independent moves to boost their revenues from bauxite up to 600%, and the International Bauxite Association was formed. At that time, aluminum companies "were more worried about the security of their supplies and what the future held," a State Department official recalls.

Yet the 11-nation IBA, stung by the steep 1975 slump in aluminum demand, so far hasn't succeeded in fulfilling some members' hopes of "organizing" world prices for the red, clay-like ore. With oil-price rises and rampant inflationary pressures of earlier years abating, several nations have begun going their own ways in taxing the commodity.

"The evidence is mounting that the major companies have largely made their peace with the countries," says C. Fred Bergsten, senior fellow with the Brookings Institution, a Washington-based research organization. He does, however, see bauxite prices rising "moderately" once world demand recovers from the recession.

Formula Status Uncertain

So far, the would-be cartel hasn't even agreed on a common-pricing formula, a device IBA backers have said is necessary to keep aluminum companies from playing off one producing country against another. The fact that a still-secret common-price formula was only "recommended"—not "approved"—by IBA's top ministers last fall means it won a two-thirds majority, but wasn't unanimously backed.

The naysayers are understood to have included Australia, the world's largest bauxite producer. While that nation's support is viewed as crucial to any effective IBA move to common pricing, it's far from guaranteed. The government that brought the country into the association was replaced by a more conservative one last fall. And Australia hasn't a federal bauxite levy, though the state of Queensland does.

The IBA members, of course, continue to cooperate in "long-term" pricing studies. "The honeymoon is over, but we still have a marriage," says Henri Guda, IBA's secretary general. One source describes the tone of the IBA executive board's first 1976 session held in Kingston, Jamaica, last month as "low-key . . . much less action-oriented on the question of pricing."

No one seems anxious to predict that a common-price strategy might emerge by November, when the top IBA ministers gather in Sierra Leone for their third annual meeting. (Members include Jamaica, Surinam, Guyana, the Dominican Republic, Haiti, Ghana, Guinea, Sierra Leone, Yugoslavia, Indonesia and Australia.)

Threat of New Sources

For one thing, new sources of ore could undermine the IBA members. Brazil plans to expand its bauxite production greatly, but to date has refused to join the group. And industry sources argue that projected costs to use alternate (nonbauxite) ores set a "ceiling" on how far bauxite prices can rise.

Meanwhile, the bauxite countries are just recovering from the effects of last year's severe decline in demand for aluminum. Bureau of Mines figures show that U.S. imports of dried bauxite last year tumbled 25% from 1974 to 10.7 million long tons.

This decline "had a significant effect on the revenues of major exporters" of bauxite to the U.S., according to the IBA's third quarterly review issued recently. But the association does contend that revenues were supported to some degree by improved aluminum ingot prices and the so-called "Jamaican formula," which first tied bauxite levies to ingot quotes.

And the outlook for bauxite revenues naturally is expected to improve as world economies strengthen. Guyana Bauxite Co., or Guybau, formed five years ago to operate the former holdings of Alcan Aluminium Ltd., expects 1976 sales to rise about $20 million, or 18%, from last year's $109.1 million, Patterson Thompson, chairman, says.

But the 1975 slump has prompted several concessions from the bauxite nations. For instance, Jamaica, the feisty price leader, has given ground on its "minimum production" requirements initiated two years ago when it boosted ore levies sharply. (These set minimum ore tonnages on which companies would be taxed, regardless of how much they actually mined.) Reynolds Metals Co., for example, last year got a 27% reduction from the 3,128,000-ton production minimum originally set for 1975.

And the size of the levies is inching upward more slowly these days. Jamaica, which originally had planned to raise its levy to 8.5% of the "realized" U.S. price of primary aluminum ingot by this year, has since negotiated to keep it at 7.5% at least through 1977.

A three-year pact valued at about $68 million recently signed between Surinam and an Aluminum Co. of America unit, negotiated against the background of the recession, calls for that country's levy to remain at the present 6% level through 1978. "We've been realistic," says John deVries, Surinam's consul general. In the U.S. "if you ask for an increase (in levy) but as a result you get a drop in production, then where are you?" he asks.

It isn't clear how fast the countries can move toward their longer-range goal of more control over bauxite facilities. Jamaica has reached preliminary agreements to take a 51% stake in bauxite mining and shipping operations of such companies as Richmond, Va.-based Reynolds and Oakland, Calif.-based Kaiser Aluminum & Chemical Corp. (38% owned by Kaiser Industries Corp.)

Pittsburgh-based Alcoa, which expects to conclude its agreement within a month, isn't denying reports from Kingston that Jamaica is seeking far less of a share in its $150 million alumina refinery than in its $30 million bauxite operation. Alumina is the intermediate product in the processing of raw bauxite ore into aluminum metal.

The success of OPEC has led to attempts to form cartels in a variety of commodities by producer countries. What obstacles must any cartel overcome in order to be successful? (The above article should give you some clues.)

Copy Cat Service Tells 'Other Side' Of Pricing Battle

By DAVID B. HILDER

James Jacobs, owner of the Copy Cat Xerox copying service in the J. August clothing store, yesterday fired another salvo in the Mass Ave Xerox copying price war.

Jacobs posted two of his employees outside J. August and Gnomon Copy on Mass Ave to distribute leaflets announcing that Copy Cat's price of two cents per copy will be guaranteed until December 31.

The two-cents-per-copy price may be extended beyond December 31, Jacobs said yesterday, but added that he may increase the price after that date if the Xerox Corporation increases the prices of supplies.

Jacob's leaflet carried the announcement of the price guarantee on one side and a copy of a leaflet that Gnomon Copy distributed last week on the other side, along with a handwritten statement that Copy Cat "will not be intimidated to raise prices to Gnomon levels."

The leaflet that Gnomon distributed last week alleged that Copy Cat was selling copies at a price below cost, so as to cut out all competition and ultimately raise its prices.

Jacobs said yesterday that his leaflet "told both sides of the story."

Since Copy Cat lowered its price and the leafletting barrages began last week, business has increased for both the copying service and the J. August store, Jacobs said yesterday.

John Sytek, vice president of Gnomon Copy, said last night Gnomon will continue to match J. August's price on loose original copy orders until December 31, but added he is not sure what Gnomon's pricing policy would be after that date.

NOTE AND QUESTIONS

This article should be read with "Xerox Price Story" which follows. Do you think the 2¢ per copy price of J. August is an attempt at predatory price cutting? If not, what other reasons can you give for the price reduction?

[65]

XEROX PRICE STORY

THE PHOENIX, FEBRUARY 9, 1971   PAGE TWENTY-ONE

Harvard Square: War of the Xerox Machines

By Vin McLellan

(PUSH TO START. Whirr *Flash* snap. Hummm . . .) The duplicating triplicating copy shops rank behind only the panhandlers and the ubiquitous newspaper hawkers in prominence among the business enterprises of the Square. It's an industry, subject to all the somersaults that add spice to Wall Street, so why should we be surprised at the first price war among the Xerox machines of Harvard Square?

While Xerox machines nestled everywhere from the Arabic Language Dept. at Harvard to the board room of the Cambridge Trust Co. do a little moonlighting, the tycoons of the market are all on Mass. Ave.: Reproductions, Copy Quik, Gnomon-Copy and Copy Cat Educational Services, Inc. The latter, which is tucked among the Arrow shirts and Chess King slacks in the J. August Clothing Store, is the shrimp of the big four, with only one machine. But Jimmy Jacobs, the gnarled old pro who owns both the store and the copy service, takes credit for starting the turmoil.

Jacobs has been running the J. August clothing store for the past 28 years. He has never been considered anything less than a shrewd merchant. His clothing store was competing against the Harvard Coop back in the years when the Coop offered a 10 per cent discount to members, but, as Jacob proudly boasts, "this store has made money every week of those 28 years!"

Short, heavy, red-faced with thinning red hair, Jacobs defends his price change from the highest Xeroxing prices in the Square to a low that all his competitors say is profitless as "another smart marketing move" of the sort that has kept him in the black "throughout my 43 years of merchandising experience — from Fifth Ave. to Harvard Square, via Howard Ave. in Roxbury."

His competitors all claim that Jacobs is carrying out a previous threat to lower his prices to where he would drive them out of business if they did not raise their prices to his then higher rates. Gnomon Copy, one of whose three Cambridge copy shops is just two doors away from the J. August Store, is the only copy center to respond by matching Jacobs' new low prices. But they made the move with considerable rancor.

When Jacobs made the price change two weeks ago, Gnomon responded by matching prices and then posting a broadside in their windows giving the "Xerox Price Story." Jacobs, Gnomon charged, "had sent word to the other Xerox services in Harvard Square that he was going to drive them all out of business . . . if they did not raise their prices to match his, which were then substantially higher than the going rate . . . Now, Jacobs has carried out his threat."

The Gnomon notice went on to explain that they had matched Jacobs' price at their Mass. Ave. shop in order not to lose customers, but that they were keeping the prices at their other two Cambridge stores at their previous prices, which they "consider to be fair and reasonable." They urged a boycott of the J. August copy shop, asserting "You may pay a higher price today, but you will insure a viable competitive situation for the future."

A couple of hours after Gnomon posted that notice, Mr. Jacobs visited his competitor to protest. As John Sytek, a Gnomon VP, remembers it, "He barged in here, mad as hell, and told one of our employees, 'You call your boss and tell him he's got five minutes to take that down or I'll photograph it and use it in a libel suit'." Gnomon management reconsidered and decided they hadn't gone far enough. They assigned one of their employees to stand in front of the J. August Store every day and pass out the Xerox Price Story leaflet. Mr. Jacobs retaliated with a movie camera, filming the leafleters. Last Thursday, when I visited the copy centers, Mr. Jacobs brought out one of his clothing salesmen and took moving pictures of one of the Gnomon people passing a leaflet to his salesman. As this was going on, one of the salesgirls from Gnomon was franticly searching for her camera to run out and photograph Mr. Jacobs photographing everyone else. When the Gnomon leafleter ran out of notices, he began modeling his clothes, Mr. Jacobs laughed and kept filming.

The management of the other two copy shops, Reproductions and Copy Quik, have so far refused to lower their prices, but their business is hurting. But both support Gnomon's charge that Jacobs tried to get them to fix their prices higher — closer to where his prices were, then the highest in the Square — and threatened to punish them by undercutting their prices if they didn't go along.

"Our prices are the same now as they were when we opened our first Gnomon shop back in '66 when we were still at M.I.T.," explains Gnomon president Adam Carley, "and prices have gone up on virtually everything since then. A rise in the prices was inevitable, but we sure weren't going to be told when and how much! We'll make our own decisions on that!"

On the very bottom of the leaflets that Jacobs is now using to announce his "new low price" there is a very silly looking copyright. It seems that when Gnomon decided to match his prices they merely took one of his leaflets, pasted a Gnomon logo over his, and Xeroxed it for their own leaflets.

Those leaflets and the price lists they crow are extremely confusing. Jacobs changed his prices from a 5-3-2 system which charged five cents for the first five, three cents for the next 20, and two cents from any further copies made from the same original to a 3-2-1 system which charged three cents for the first five, two for the next 15, and one cent for any more made from the same original.

What that Greek formula means is that while prior to his cut in price a customer paid 25 cents for five copies (most of his competitors charged 17 cents), he would now pay 15 cents. For 50 copies, he would have charged $1.35 under his old prices (his competitors between five and 20 cents less), the new prices demand only 75 cents.

The management of Gnomon Copy expect a libel suit, but feel that they're on solid ground. Mr. Jacobs won't say right out whether he plans to sue although he implies that "because I feel sorry for the crybabies" he might "let it pass." Meanwhile, Dick Broughton, the owner of Reproductions, a casual young shaggy-haired businessman who doesn't look like the former Xerox salesman he is, says he is considering a law suit against Jacobs because, according to his calculations, Jacobs is selling below cost, a competition tactic the law frowns upon.

Last fall, the Reproductions copy center instituted a price out from the 5-3-2 system to a 4-3-2 price list. Broughton said that soon after he had put up posters announcing the price change he was visited by Mr. Jacobs who said, "I don't want to tell you how to run your business, but if you go to 4-3-2, I'm going to 3-2-1." Broughton said he had to revoke the price change. "Look, man, I just know I couldn't afford that . . ." He still can't afford that sort of pricing, he says. Bob Chilton, one of the owners of Copy Quik says he's in the same bind. Chilton says his current prices "are established so that we can make a very small profit — we'd lose money if we matched Jacob's prices. I believe he's losing money to get us! (He) tried to control prices in the square. He tried to force everyone to raise their prices and when they didn't go along he did just what he threatened — tried to drive everyone else out."

Mr. Jacobs, of course, said he just came to the conclusion that "maybe we were a little overboard with our prices," and readjusted them. He denies all charges of attempted price fixing; "that is just a crybaby tactic on their part . . ." as to the charge that he's taking a loss, he replies, "Do I look like a philastraphist or a gypsy? I have a hell of a responsibility here. J. August Clothing has been here since 1891. It's my responsibility as a merchant to get the best possible buys to the customers and make a profit. And I'm a hell of a good merchant!"

Reprinted with permission of the *Boston Phoenix* and Gnomon Copy.

[66]

Unit of R.J. Reynolds Boosts Cigaret Prices

By a WALL STREET JOURNAL *Staff Reporter*

WINSTON-SALEM, N.C. — R. J. Reynolds Tobacco Co., a subsidiary of R. J. Reynolds Industries Inc., said it will boost prices on its cigaret brands 75 cents per 1,000, effective immediately.

All the major domestic cigaret makers now have announced increases in a round of boosts that was begun nearly two weeks ago by Loews Corp.'s Lorillard division.

Reynolds said it also will increase its anticipation allowance to wholesalers and direct buyers who·pay within 10 days, thus partially offsetting the effect of the increase.

Most cigaret makers make similar incentive payments, although Reynolds is the only one to announce an increase in the allowance in conjunction with its price increase.

Reynolds, which has been giving a 3% discount to early-pay customers, said it's increasing this to 3.25%.

TIMING OF CHANGES IN PRICES OF 99% PLUS PRIMARY ALUMINUM INGOT, THREE LEADING COMPANIES, 1950–1956

Price	Alcoa	Reynolds Metals	Kaiser
$.175	May 22, 1950	May 23, 1950	May 25, 1950
.190	Sept. 25, 1950	Sept. 29, 1950	Sept. 28, 1950
.200	Aug. 4, 1952	Aug. 4, 1952	Aug. 4, 1952
.205	Jan. 23, 1953	Jan. 23, 1953	Jan. 22, 1953
.215	July 15, 1953	July 20, 1953	July 20, 1953
.222	Aug. 5, 1954	Aug. 6, 1954	Aug. 6, 1954
.232	Jan. 13, 1955	Jan. 10, 1955	Jan. 12, 1955
.244	Aug. 1, 1955	Aug. 6, 1955	Aug. 2, 1955
.259	Mar. 29, 1956	Mar. 27, 1956	Mar. 26, 1956

Source: United States v. Aluminum Company of America, 153 F. Supp. 151

QUESTIONS

Is it just coincidence that once one major cigaret (or aluminum) producer raised prices, all the others followed suit? Why or why not? What does this indicate about the market structure?

THE DECLINING
VALUE
OF COLLEGE GOING

by Richard Freeman and J. Herbert Hollomon

Center for Policy Alternatives, Massachusetts Institute of Technology

For decades the American higher educational system has both provided individuals with training and education promising high earnings and occupational status, and supplied society with skilled specialists and white-collar workers. In the 1950s and 1960s in particular, the job market for college graduates was exceptionally strong; education was a major means to socioeconomic mobility and national economic growth. With a minority of young Americans—albeit an increasingly large one—attending college, and a growing demand for the educated, the financial rewards for the college trained were sizable and stimulated many to extend their education from 12 to 16 or more years of formal schooling. Spurred by the demand for college training, the higher educational system was significantly expanded, and many more millions enrolled than ever before. With a bull market, there was little incentive to examine the value of college education carefully: Whatever it was that was being taught was paying off in good jobs for graduates. The response was simply to expand higher education—to open the door to larger numbers of people, including disadvantaged minorities.

This golden age of higher education came to an abrupt end at the outset of the 1970s, when the 25-year boom in the college job market withered into a major market bust. For the first time in recent history, new bachelor's graduates began to have difficulty obtaining jobs, and the relative in-

> ## About MIT's Center for Policy Alternatives
>
> Begun in 1972, the Center formulates policy analyses of alternatives available to governments, industry, education, and individuals in meeting complex societal problems here and abroad, and provides objective assessments of the consequences of present policies and practices.

come of college workers fell significantly. As James O'Toole pointed out in the May and June issues of *Change*, we have now arrived at a point where a growing number of people may be destined to remain underemployed or—by implication—overeducated. More important, perhaps, for policymakers and every educator in the country is the fundamental question of whether we are dealing with relatively short-term market phenomena or with a long-term change in the functional composition of American society. Obviously, institutions, individual careers, and professions can more easily survive cyclical ups and downs than long-term declining trends that will stabilize at some later year at a far lower plateau. Relatively permanent changes are likely to require substantial alterations in the higher educational system, and in attitudes toward the relationship between education and work, social mobility, and the social value of college and university education.

Extent of the Downturn

It is important to recognize that the market turnaround of the seventies is a far-reaching, unprecedented development of sizable dimensions. By all relevant measures, the economic status of college graduates is deteriorating, with employment prospects for the young declining exceptionally sharply.

From 1969, the last good year in the college job market, to 1975, the starting salaries of male graduates in industry, having increased rapidly in the previous decade, dropped sharply, both in real terms and relative to the earnings of other workers. College Placement Council data show a decrease of 23 percent in the real starting pay for men with social science or humanities degrees; a fall of 21 percent in the real pay for beginning BS mathematics majors; and of 17 percent for beginning electrical engineers with doctorates. Declines in real rates of pay of such magnitude have not been experienced by other workers and constitute a sharp break with past patterns of change (Figure 1).

The ratio of college-graduate to high-school-graduate incomes—quite stable since World War II—also dropped in the early 1970s. In 1969, full-time male workers with four years of college earned 53 percent more than male workers with four years of high school; in 1973, 40 percent more. Among 25-34-year-old workers the drop was even sharper. A 39 percent college premium dwindled to 23 percent.

As a result of the decline in relative incomes and starting salaries and in the face of continued increases in tuition and fees, the rate of return on the college investment has fallen significantly. According to one set of estimates, the return dropped from 11-12 percent in 1969 to 7-8 percent in 1974. A decrease of this magnitude is unprecedented.

In some graduate fields, the decrease in the relative income of starting workers is even more severe than in undergraduate specialties. Figure 2 shows this decrease in terms of the ratio of the master's salaries to bachelor's graduates in engineering. The figure also indicates, however, some exceptions to this pattern, notably in business administration.

With respect to employment, the number of professional and managerial jobs has begun to level off as a percentage of all jobs in the 1970s, after a century of phenomenal growth. In 1969, 24.0 percent of all jobs were professional or managerial; in 1974, 24.8 percent. Had the number of professional and managerial jobs increased at the same rate as in the past, 27.5 percent of all workers would have been employed as professionals or managers in 1974. Even more strikingly, the ratio of these college-level jobs to the total number of graduates dropped by about 2.8 percent per

annum in the 1969-74 period.

New college graduates are having severe problems obtaining desirable work.* Over 30 percent of the graduating men and 25 percent of the women in the class of 1972 were holding nonprofessional, nonmanagerial jobs in the early seventies, compared with just over 10 percent of graduates in a roughly similar status in the class of 1958 (Figure 3). Between 1969 and 1974, the relative number of male college graduates working as salesmen and the proportion of female graduates employed in clerical positions both increased by 30 percent. About one third of the male and two thirds of the

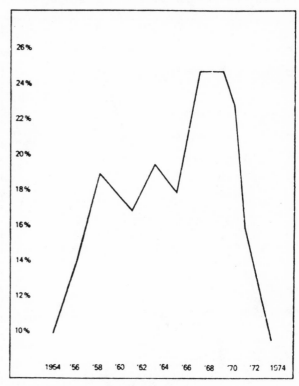

Figure 1. Starting salary advantages of college graduates over average wage and salary earnings.

female graduates have had to accept positions unrelated to their college majors in the seventies, compared with 10 percent of men and 13 percent of women in the early 1960s.

Many young college workers have also had difficulty obtaining any work upon graduation. In October 1972, before the economy entered the serious recession of the mid-seventies, 9.3 percent of the class of 1972 lacked work of any kind—15.4 percent of those who had majored in humanities; 16.0 percent of those who majored in social sci-

---

* This analysis views college graduates in aggregate. In certain fields there were still advantages and opportunities. In engineering, for example, for very special reasons, starting salaries have not fallen since 1968 in real terms.

ences. Again, historic comparison reveals the unprecedented nature of this development. Barely 1 percent of the class of 1958 was unemployed at the outset of the 1960s. By October 1972, the rate of unemployment for graduates in the class of 1972 (9.3 percent) stood far in excess of the national average for workers (5.6 percent) and above that for high school graduates of about the same age (7.7 percent). Although less dramatic, there was an analogous increase in the rate of unemployment among all college graduates and among those employed in professional and managerial jobs. In 1969, 0.9 percent of college graduates, 1.3

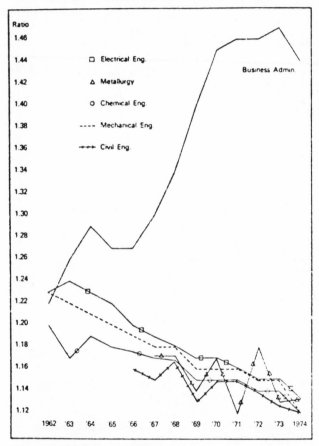

Figure 2. Starting salary advantages, master's vs. bachelor's, for selected professions.

percent of professionals, and 0.9 percent of managers lacked employment compared with an economywide average of 3.5 percent. Between 1969 and 1974, these rates rose to 2.0 percent (college graduates), 2.3 percent (professionals), and 1.8 percent (managers) while the overall rate increased less rapidly to 5.6 percent. Finally, the length of unemployment among college graduates in the seventies exceeded that of other workers. Thirty-two percent of unemployed male graduates were without work for 15 weeks or more in 1973 compared with just 27.5 percent of typical unemployed workers. In short, the mass media have not

exaggerated the situation: In the brief span of about five years, the college job market has gone from a major boom to a major bust.

In response to the dearth of economic opportunities for college graduates, there has been a marked decline in the proportion of young men choosing to enroll in college.* Between 1969 and 1974 the fraction of 18-19-year-old men enrolled as students in higher education fell from 44.0 percent to 33.4 percent—a remarkable switch in the historic trend for increased college entrance. Among young women, on the other hand, the percentage enrolled has leveled off, but not fallen.

The decrease among men appears to have occurred, moreover, in all social strata, although it has been most pronounced among lower-middle-class families. Large numbers of young people, for the first time, are likely to obtain less schooling and potentially lower occupational status than their parents.

There are, however, two major exceptions to this striking national phenomenon of lower enrollments. Young blacks, according to Bureau of the Census data, who first began attending in large numbers in the sixties, continued to increase their representation in higher education in the 1970s, substantially narrowing the black/white gap in enrollments. In 1969, 236,000 black men were in college; in 1975, 422,000, bringing the black share of male students from 5 to 9 percent. As a percentage of 18-19-year-olds, black male enrollments increased slightly over the same period, from 23 percent to 25 percent, despite the overall drop in the proportion of young men in college.

The differential pattern of black and white enrollments is readily attributable to differences in labor market incentives. While opportunities deteriorated in the seventies for white graduates, the position of black graduates appears to have improved significantly. The share of black graduates obtaining managerial jobs—from which blacks had historically been excluded—jumped from 5 percent in 1964 to 11 percent in 1969 and then to 19 percent in 1973, while white representation in management was relatively unchanged. The incomes of black male college graduates increased by 104 percent in the sixties compared to 67 percent for white graduates. In the 1969-73 period of market decline, incomes of black graduates rose by 32 percent while those of white graduates increased by just 20 percent. Perhaps most importantly, the starting salaries of black college graduates rose to parity with those of whites in the sixties and early seventies, after decades of being

* The evidence that some student respond to changes in economic incentives in their decisions to go to college is presented in some of the references at the end of the article.

substantially lower. Estimates of the rate of return on college investments for blacks are difficult to make, as there is considerable uncertainty about whether parity among the young will be maintained. But even pessimistic calculations suggest higher rates for blacks than for whites in the 1970s: a return in 1974, for example, on the order of 11-12 percent compared with 8.5 percent estimated for college graduates as a whole.

Enrollments also increased among a second group—older men and women, aged 30-34 or over 35, who have traditionally attended college in relatively small numbers. In 1969, 536,000 people aged 30-34 enrolled in college; in 1974, 720,000; 5.1 percent of men in that age bracket attended in the former year, compared with 6.5 percent in the latter. As for those 35 and over, between 1972 (when data were first obtained for this age group) and 1974, enrollments jumped by 30 percent to about one million. The majority of these people attended part-time (as might be expected given the likelihood of their having family responsibilities) and enrolled in vocational programs designed to help their careers.

There are several factors behind the movement of older people into college: increased recognition of the need for retraining in fields of rapid technological progress by companies that provide special programs and funds for occupational education; declines in the number of children per family, which leave time for other activities; special recruitment efforts by colleges hard pressed for students; changes in ideas about the value of education; and the short hours and unemployment of the recession of 1974-75, which make it less costly to switch from work to school activities.

To the extent that long-run rather than cyclical factors underlie the observed changes, the rise in adult enrollments could portend a major change in the age distribution of college students, particularly in the 1980s, when the number of the young will decline for demographic reasons. An enormous movement of adults into higher education would be needed to save the college and university system from the expected fall in student population. Even with the increases of the 1970s, such an increase seems unlikely, though our knowledge of the enrollment decisions of older people is currently limited.

Temporary, Cyclical, or Long-Run?

Analysis of the causes of the seventies' turnaround suggests that the market developments represent a major break with the past and are not simply cyclical or temporary phenomena. Underlying the collapse of the college job market is what promises to be a long-term change in the supply-

demand balance due to several factors. On the demand side, the growth of most sectors of the economy, using a relatively large number of college graduates, has leveled off after two decades or so of rapid growth. While the growth of certain other sectors also employing significant numbers of college graduates (such as finance and professional services) has not declined, it has been insufficient to maintain the pace of employment. From 1960 to 1969 employment in college manpower intensive industries, in total, increased by 4.4 percent, compared to an increase in other industries of 2.0 percent. From 1969 to 1974, the growth rate of college manpower intensive sectors declined to 2.8

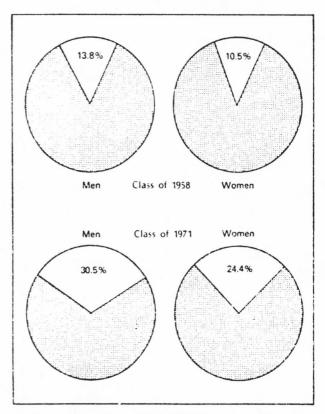

Figure 3. Percentages of college graduates entering nonmanagerial and nonprofessional jobs.

percent while other industries continued to increase at 2.0 percent. Similarly, the proportion of the gross national product (GNP) allocated to two activities that employ large numbers of college trained people, education and R&D, also declined at the turn of the decade. Between 1964 and 1973, the R&D share of GNP fell from 3.0 percent to 2.4 percent; between 1971 and 1973 the education share of GNP was off from 8.0 to 7.6 percent. As a result of the shift in the composition of output and employment, the long-term growth of demand for college workers *decelerated* substantially in the seventies.

Coincident with the leveling off in demand was

an extraordinary increase in the number of new graduates seeking work—the result of the large numbers that were of college age and chose to go to college and graduate school in the 1960s. While the number of students increased rapidly throughout the 1960s, the number actually graduating and seeking work did not increase by as much—largely because many chose to obtain graduate training in the booming market. With the decline of the seventies, the proportion enrolling in graduate schools has fallen, while those who sought graduate degrees four or five years earlier have finally entered the market, with the result that

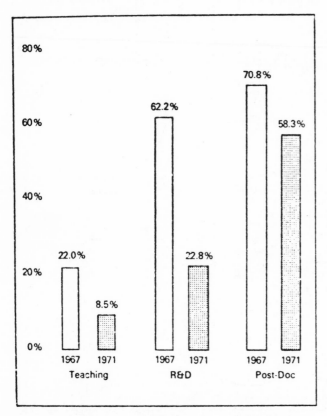

Figure 4. Percentage of PhDs taking academic jobs in institutions of equal or higher rank than their graduate schools (by Cartter rankings).

supply has increased sharply. Estimates of the number of new BAs seeking work, obtained by subtracting those going to graduate school (but ignoring the movement of older people into graduate training), suggest that the number of new male BAs "on the job market" increased by 8 percent per annum (relative to the male work force) from 1968 to 1973, compared to a modest 1.75 percent per annum in the sixties. In addition, the flow of new graduates was so much greater throughout the period than the number of retiring BAs that the total supply of college-trained workers increased rapidly as a fraction of the work

force—a development almost certain to continue into the 1980s due to the continued small number of college graduates nearing retirement age.

This combination of deceleration of growth in demand and massive increase in supply in the 1970s—not the overall recession or some other relatively short-term development—underlies the remarkable turnaround in the college job market and appears to have caused the decline in the fraction of young males entering college. Some young people considering higher education are responding to the decline in job opportunities and the declining rate of return on the educational investment. Responses to changing incentives have been found in a wide variety of professions—law, physics, engineering, accounting—and for the aggregate of college students. These results do not imply that educational decisions of all people are motivated by economic conditions, only that a large number are sensitive to the job market.

As for the future, the supply-demand analysis of the market outlined above has been used to predict the economic status of graduates for the next decade or so. Formal econometric forecasts, using the Freeman-Center for Policy Alternatives "Recursive Adjustment Model" of the college job market (which relates supply to economic incentives and their interaction with demand) suggest that even if the whole economy reverts to full employment, this gloomy picture for college graduates is likely to continue. Barring unforeseen increases in demand for college graduates, their relative economic status is expected to deteriorate moderately or remain at the present depressed level until the end of the decade.*

In the late seventies and early eighties, however, the market is expected to improve, particularly for young graduates, as the supply of new bachelor's degree recipients diminishes due to declining enrollments in response to the depressed market and to declines in the size of the college-age pool. This improvement will raise the proportion of the young choosing college and ameliorate some of the effects of the declining number of college-age people on enrollments. In the market as a whole, the situation is expected to stabilize or improve in the late eighties, when the total number of college-trained workers relative to the labor force reaches an approximate equilibrium. The portion of the work force made up of college graduates will increase until the latter part of the 1980s, despite cutbacks in enrollment, because the small number of retiring graduates will maintain supply pressures until that period. The key

*Again, this is not so in all fields. Engineering and computer science will have selectively good markets and will continue to attract students for the next few years.

element in these forecasts is the responsive supply behavior of young people, whose decisions are anticipated to equilibrate the market by reducing the supply of college workers. If the proportion of the young that elects higher education does not, for whatever reason, change in the expected manner, the depressed market is likely to last throughout the 1980s.

Forecasts such as these must, of course, be treated cautiously, for the track record in projecting changes in the economic value of schooling is not good. Seymour Harris, for example, writing in 1949, expected the fifties and sixties to be decades of market glut: "A large proportion of the potential college students within the next 20 years are doomed to disappointment after graduating as the number of correlated openings (in professional jobs) will be substantially less than the numbers seeking them."

Harris's predictions did not come to pass because of the large increase in demand for graduates in the fifties and sixties due, according to our analysis, to the shift in the composition of industrial employment, a spurt in R&D spending, and demographic changes that led to the expansion of the education sector. Prior to the market turnaround of the 1970s, human capital economists were concerned with reasons for the stability in the ratios of the incomes of educated to less educated workers, and sought relatively long-term or permanent rather than temporary reasons for this pattern. Provisos and equivocation notwithstanding, if the analysis is reasonably on target, the economic value of college will be smaller than in the past, with important consequences for higher education.

SOMETHING TO THINK ABOUT

As you read this article, ask yourself to what extent the results that have been reported can be explained in terms of the theory of demand and the supply of factors.

Commodities

Housing Dispute Spurs Michigan Farmers to Switch to Machines from Migrant Help

BY NORMAN PEARLSTINE

Staff Reporter of the Wall Street Journal

LANSING, Mich.–Michigan growers of fruit and vegetables expect a good harvest this summer. But for the thousands of migrant workers who are expected to stream into the state to help harvest the crops, the pickings are likely to be slim.

Growers are stepping up their use of machines to harvest crops, so there will be fewer jobs available, according to farm-labor authorities here. Housing for the migrants will also be scarcer this summer, mainly because of unwillingness or inability of growers to comply with tougher Federal and state housing standards.

With abundant help from migrant workers (only California uses more of them), Michigan has become the nation's largest producer of red tart cherries, dry beans, pickly cucumbers, blueberries and hothouse rhubarb. Migrants also help gather the state's big crops of apples, grapes, sugar beets, soybeans and potatoes.

But higher labor costs have prompted many growers here and elsewhere throughout the country to switch to mechanized harvesting in recent years, lessening demand for migrant workers. That trend has intensified in the last two years, as government agencies have implemented stricter housing regulations for growers participating in their migrant-worker placement programs.

Many growers say that unfavorable publicity about housing condition for migrants on some farms prompted them to close down migrant-labor camps and to switch to mechanization. "It might be cheaper for me to continue using migrant help for a few more years," says one western Michigan fruit grower, "but mechanization is the trend of the future. And no matter what kind of housing I provide, I'm going to be criticized for mistreating migrants so I might as well switch now," he adds.

No Variances

Under Federal regulations, growers can't use an interstate farm-labor service unless they meet housing standards set by the Labor Department. These regulations allow for variances from the standards if they don't create a health or safety hazard. Michigan growers assert that last winter the Labor Department's regional officer in Chicago decided against allowing any variances.

Several growers in western Michigan reacted by circulating petitions throughout the state demanding that variances be granted and that the state and Federal government provide aid to growers who had to make large capital expenditures to upgrade their migrant camps. Other growers exerted political pressure on the legislators in Michigan and Washington to get the standards relaxed. About 10,000 persons signed the petitions and in mid-April officials of the Labor Department in Washington agreed that variances should be allowed.

Many other growers, however, simply decided that they wouldn't participate in the interstate service this year and wouldn't submit their housing to the scrutiny of officials. Joseph C. Kaspar, Chicago regional director for the Farm-Labor and Rural-Manpower Service, says that variances and interstate orders have been granted to almost any grower who has asked for them. But there have been relatively few applications, he adds.

Sharp Reductions

The lack of work contracts and the relative scarcity of jobs has been particularly severe in Saginaw-Bay City area of the state, whrere many sugar-beet growers mechanized this year and closed their migrant camps. Roy Fuentes, a member of the Office of Economic Opportunity here, says that the Saginaw-Bay City area "is very short of migrant housing," and he adds that "it will be a pretty rough summer" for migrants throughout the state.

Donald E. Holtzman, a South Haven blueberry farmer, says that he used as many as 150 migrants three years ago to help harvest his crop, but that he plans to use fewer than a dozen this summer.

State and Federal officials estimate that mechanization could eliminate from 6,000 to 10,000 jobs in Michigan this summer that were previously done by migrants. Norman Papsdorf, chief of the Michigan Department of Health's agricultural labor-camps unit, which licenses all the state's migrant labor camps, says license applications are down 11% so far this summer to 1,575 from 1,775 a year ago.

Nonetheless, approximately 50,000 migrant workers, mostly Mexican-Americans from southwest Texas, are expected to come into Michigan looking for work this summer. That's about the same number that came through last year. Their slimmer chances of finding available work and shelter have been aggravated by an apparent breakdown here in the Federal-state program for interstate recruitment of migrants.

In recent years more than half of the migrants coming into the state have been recruited and placed in jobs and living camps by the Michigan Employment Security Commission, a Federally supported state agency that works closely with the Laobr Department. Last year the commission's farm-labor rural-manpower service arranged jobs and housing for 27,163 workers. But this year commission officials say that "we're only going to place about 7,000 or 8,000 workers." The rest of the migrants coming into the state will have to finf their own work and shelter.

The growers' decision against using the interstate service this summer stems primarily from the heated battle they had with state and Federal authorities earlier this year over interpretation of the Federal housing standards.

Mr. Fuentes says that the state may try to go into the housing business itself, leasing accommodations to migrants. In addition, the Michigan Economic Opportunity Office has announced that it will set up at least 17 area councils throughout the state to establish a number of centers providing food, medical and dental care for migrants.

Meanwhile, agriculture experts here say they see good crop prospects. Weather has been good and pollination of fruit trees successful throughout most of the state. Although it is too early to forecast crop prices, most authorities say that this year's crop revenue should match last year's respectable showing, when the state's growers received about $70 million for their fruit and about $57 million for their vegetables.

The Michigan Crop Reporting Service, a statistical bureau supported by the state and Federal agriculture departments, has forecast that this year's tart-cherry crop will be about 1,000 tons less than the 106,000 tons harvested last year, while the sweet cherry crop is predicted to increase 1,000 tons to 23,000 tons. Bigger peach and pear crops also are predicted.

The reporting services hasn't yet made its forecast for commercial apples, the state's most valuable fruit crop. But some industry sources are looking for this year's apple harvest to be at least as good as last year when about 680 million pounds of apples worth about $27 million were picked. Michigan ranks third among apple-producing states.

QUESTIONS

(1) Explain, using the least-cost condition, the effect of stricter housing standards on migrant employment.

(2) Who do you see as being helped by this stricter housing standard? Who do you see as being hurt?

Cheap Mexican Labor Attracts U.S. Companies to the Border

By JAMES P. STERBA
Special to The New York Times

BROWNSVILLE, Tex., May 9—The 35 women who sort and box shrimp at Tex-Mex Cold Storage Inc. are quick with their hands. With the help of machines, they can grade and package for freezing about 6,000 pounds of shrimp an hour. Their base pay is $2.30 an hour; their take-home pay: $2.12 an hour.

The 160 women who peel and devein shrimp at Camarones Selectos S.A., just across the border in Matamoros, Mexico, are also quick with their hands. Without machines, they can remove the shells and back veins from about 2,000 pounds of shrimp an hour. Their base pay: 99 cents an hour; their take-home pay: 65 cents an hour.

It is that basic disparity in wages that both lures Mexican workers into the United States and propels United States labor-intensive industries into Mexico. United States labor union officials charge that both movements are costing United States workers jobs at a time when unemployment rates remain high.

Hundreds of United States companies have closed factories in other parts of the country over the last decade and set up new plants along the border to take advantage of low labor costs on the Mexican side and abundant minimum-wage labor on the United States side. The border, in fact, has become an open sore in the Carter Administration's efforts to put Americans back to work, formulate a new immigration policy and deal with pressures for trade embargoes.

Although many companies have simply moved their labor-intensive jobs to such places as South Korea, Taiwan and Hong Kong, American union officials have focused much of their attention on Mexican workers, saying that they in particular are stripping jobs away from American workers.

But a look at the shrimp industry around Brownsville, which calls itself "Shrimp Capital of the World," shows a different picture. Virtually all the jobs requiring labor are performed by men and women of Mexican origin. Some are United States citizens. Many are Mexican citizens living legally on this side of the border. Some are Mexican citizens who live in Mexico and commute to jobs here or work in factories set up in Mexico by United States companies.

Shrimp boat owners and shrimp company processors contend that they simply cannot find many United States citizens who are willing to work at jobs, which are often part time, for wages at the Federal minimum of $2.30 an hour or slightly higher. At the same time, they say there is an abundant supply of Mexicans who are eager to take those jobs and grateful to get them.

But for the most labor-intensive chores of peeling and deveining shrimp, processors avoid even United States minimum wages by trucking their shrimp across the border into Mexico. Wages of 99 cents an hour seem paltry by United standards, but they are above average for workers in Mexico.

Americans and Mexicans who run processing plants, as well as a variety of other factories on the Mexican side of the border, contend that these plants actually save jobs in the United States. Without them, they contend, many American companies would be forced to move their entire operation to foreign soil in order to remain competitive.

To illustrate how this works, one can follow the circuitous path of a load of shrimp caught the other day in the Gulf of Mexico.

With a permit that costs $2,006 a year, United States shrimp boats can net shrimp in Mexican waters. The boats have Three-man crews of a captain, rig man and header. Many of the rig men are Mexican-Americans. Most of the headers, who remove the heads from shrimp and clean the boats, are Mexicans.

The boats from Brownsville are unloaded usually by Mexican workers. Boat maintenance and cleanup crews at the port are also usually Mexicans.

Shrimp Processor's View

Lawrence Touchet, manager of Gulf Shrimp Processors, hires 50 to 60 Mexicans in the peak season to unload the boats, ice the shrimp and load them onto trucks.

"I don't care how many people are supposed to be out of work, you just can't get Americans to do this work," he said.

The shrimp are then trucked to Tex-Mex Cold Storage for sorting, sizing, boxing and freezing. Ed Walker, the company's production manager, agrees with Mr. Touchet.

QUESTIONS

(1) Use the "least-cost" condition to explain why producers of shrimp in the U.S. will use more machines relative to labor.

(2) What do you think would happen if the U.S. minimum wage law was repealed?

On financing future schlock

Mortgage interest rates at last have descended part way out of the stratosphere, setting hammers to tap-tapping again in housing developments. The long blight on home construction is over, and house-hunters heading for new subdivisions and suburban tracts this spring will find that real estate developers are not only building houses again but are expanding into the appliance and furnishings business in a big way.

Builders now sell 25 or 30 per cent of all major appliances, according to trade sources, doubling their share of those sales a decade ago. Only a range top and an oven used to come already installed in a new house. Now many large national construction companies are offering dishwashers, washing machines, dryers. garbage disposers. refrigerators and, most recently, trash compactors. The Census Bureau reports that half of all homes built in 1969 came equipped with dishwashers, 10 per cent with refrigerators and 2 per cent with washers and dryers. According to a study by Westinghouse Electric Corporation, the average new house in 1970 included 3.1 major appliances and, by 1980, will include 4.4 major appliances.

Wall-to-wall carpeting. usually with no finished wood flooring beneath it, is another standard feature in many tract houses. The Federal Housing Administration (FHA), which, together with the Veterans Administration. insures the mortgages of one-third of new houses. permits builders to lay carpet directly over the subflooring, as long as the carpet meets FHA quality standards. Why require expensive hardwood floors, the reasoning goes, when almost every homeowner immediately carpets them over.

Lower appliance prices

Builders claim that appliances and carpeting help to sell houses. They also claim they can offer those items at much lower prices than you would pay for identical brands and models in retail stores, and there is some truth to that. Home-building has become a big business with big purchasing power. Kaufman and Broad, Inc., of Los Angeles, built 5700 one-family houses last year and expects to put up more than 7000 this year. The Larwin Group, a subsidiary of the giant CNA Financial conglomerate, built almost 8000 dwelling units in 1971. The National Appliance and Radio-TV Dealers Association complains that big builders are able to negotiate special deals with manufacturers and to sell appliances to home buyers for at least one-third below store prices.

Along with low prices goes the convenience of moving into a fully equipped house without having to shop for appliances and carpets. and. more important, without having to put up much extra money. This convenience is not unadulterated. For one thing, while the builder may offer a choice of models, he usually sells only one manufacturer's brand. selected less for its quality. perhaps, than for its negotiated wholesale price. The builder's brand may not be the one you would have picked. And as CU's brand Ratings and Frequency-of-Repair data often bring out, there can be significant differences in estimated overall quality and maintenance costs. Furthermore. builders in general have not won good reputations for honoring their warranties.

Economics of financing

The economics of financing such things as washing machines and carpets with a mortgage should also be seriously weighed. Consider. for instance. that the average mortgage on a new house has a term of 27 years. Yet the average life of a washing machine is said to be 10 years. of a dryer 12 years. a dishwasher 10 years. and a refrigerator 15 years, including second-hand use. The life expectancy of carpeting is utterly unpredictable but may be considerably shorter than that of an appliance. This much is plain: A mortgaged appliance or carpet may have to be replaced before it has been anywhere near paid for.

In the simple arithmetic of interest costs, a mortgage appears to be a very expensive way to finance home furnishings. To illustrate. let's assume that the builder is offering a washing machine. clothes dryer and automatic dishwasher. Their total price at an appliance store is $675. The builder's price is one-third less. $450. Let's further assume a mortgage of average length. 27 years, at the national average interest rate (last December) of 7³⁄₁ per cent. Finally. let's compare the mortgage finance charges with those for the same appliances purchased at the store's price and with the store's two-year, 15 per cent installment contract. Here are the figures:

	Cost from store	Cost from builder
Purchase price	$675	$ 450
Finance charge	110	625
Total	$785	$1075

At those terms, the appliances would cost $290 more from the builder than from the store.

Let's take a set of terms more favorable to the builder's

case. In some parts of the country last winter, mortgage money was available at 7 per cent. Some stores, meanwhile, were charging 18 per cent interest on a two-year appliance contract. The consumer's arithmetic would look like this:

	Cost from store	Cost from builder
Purchase price	$675	$ 450
Finance charge	134	553
Total	$809	$1003

At those terms, the appliances would cost an extra $194 from the builder.

It can be said in favor of the builder's deal that mortgage payments after a number of years will probably be made with inflation-cheapened dollars. Unfortunately, inflation won't stem the rapidly depreciating value of carpets and appliances, even though the value of the house may appreciate handsomely.

Turnover rate

The fact is, houses change hands an average of once every seven or eight years, and so the average homeowner doesn't pay the full finance charges on his mortgage. He sells his house, uses some of the proceeds to pay off his mortgage and, more than likely, plunks down the rest as down payment on another house. His mortgage payments over the first eight years of ownership consisted mostly of interest. Hardly any principle was paid off: that is the nature of a long-term mortgage. Thus the homeowner finds himself still owing the mortgage lender almost the whole purchase price of any carpets and appliances lumped into the mortgage. Now used and worn, they are hardly worth the price of moving them

to his new house. The people buying his old house, however, may not want used carpets or appliances and certainly won't pay for them.

Moral: It is expensive to buy appliances, carpets and other home furnishings on credit, no matter where you finance them. Take advantage of the builder's low-priced furnishings if you wish—but only after making sure they are less expensive than from a store—and try to make a large enough cash down payment to cover their price.

A modular future?

The selling trend is going very much in the direction of lumping all sorts of short-lived furnishings into the mortgage. Builders at the Houston home show last January told Home Furnishings Daily they will include in the mortgage package "anything and everything." They mentioned not only carpets and appliances but also draperies and hardware.

Two of the biggest developers, Levitt & Sons and the Larwin Group, already operate furniture stores on some of their building sites, although furniture is not yet being included in their mortgages. The FHA, for its part, seems to be loosening rather than tightening restrictions on items includable in the mortgages it insures.

The trend reaches its present zenith with mobile homes, many of which come completetly furnished and financed. The future, as predicted by some students of the construction industry, will be dominated by factory-built modules—ready-made rooms with furniture, rugs and appliances already installed. Turn-key houses, they are called, because the buyer has only to turn the key and start living in them. And paying for them, as the English say, on the never-never.

QUESTIONS

Consumer Reports is supposed to be the consumer's sage protector. Would you follow this author's advice and buy the appliance from the store? What has the author ignored in his analysis?

Quick Adjustment

Fast-Food Chains Act To Offset the Effects Of Minimum-Pay Rise

Fewer Hours, Higher Prices, More Automation Due; But Layoffs Are Avoided

How Slow-Cookers Cut Costs

By PAUL INGRASSIA
Staff Reporter of THE WALL STREET JOURNAL

HANOVER PARK, Ill.—Cheryl Anders, an 18-year-old part-time hostess at a Kentucky Fried Chicken restaurant here, won't be losing her job after all.

Earlier this year, executives in the $16 billion-a-year fast-food industry tried to forestall the increase in the federal minimum wage to $2.65 an hour from $2.30 by warning that many people like Miss Anders would have to be laid off. The increase was enacted anyway, and yet few layoffs are likely.

Unions that lobbied for the increase, on the other hand, predicted that people like Miss Anders would get a well-deserved 15% pay increase. And that generally won't be happening, either.

[A]

Miss Anders's employer, the KFC subsidiary of Heublein Inc., for example, is tightening work schedules at the stores it owns to help offset the effects of the higher wages. In the case of Miss Anders, she will now be working 18 hours a week instead of 23, and earning about $48 a week after Jan. 1, down from the $53 a week she has been averaging.

"I don't mind getting fewer hours because I have more time for other things," she says. "But some people in the store don't like it."

Coping With Costs

[B]

KFC's tighter scheduling is but one example of the steps that fast-food chains are taking to deal with the higher labor costs. Also being considered or implemented are such things as more automation—and, not surprisingly, higher prices. [B ends here.]

The fast-food companies aren't the only employers with a lot of workers paid the minimum wage, by any means. The Labor Department estimates that 4.5 million workers will be eligible for the automatic increase to $2.65 an hour on Jan. 1, or about 4.5% of the U.S. labor force. Besides fast-food and other restaurants, the industries feeling the greatest impact will be department and grocery stores, hotels, service stations, cleaners and custodial services. Low-wage manufacturers such as textile and apparel companies will also be hit, the Labor Department says.

The new law calls for further increases in the minimum wage, to $2.90 an hour in 1979, $3.10 in 1980 and $3.35 in 1981. Some states, moreover, have minimums above the federal level (see story on page 13).

The fast-food industry, which has seen a tripling of sales since 1970, was clearly alarmed by the potential effects of the new pay increase, as most of its employes earn little more than the minimum wage. Last summer, when the legislation was taking shape, executives of the hamburger and chicken chains were forecasting that hundreds of thousands of teen-agers would be thrown out of work.

Shorter Hours Considered

But such giants as KFC, McDonald's and Hardee's now say they don't plan any layoffs. Instead, for the fast-food industry and its customers, the net result of the minimum-wage increase will generally be that the late-night hamburger probably will become a little harder to find and a few cents costlier to buy.

Not that the pay raise won't cost the U.S. economy any jobs. Even the Carter administration, which strongly backed the increase, estimated it could cost some 90,000 jobs through 1981. But the fast-food chains are planning to avoid layoffs with selective price increases, massive marketing efforts to increase sales volume and technological gains in the kitchen to boost productivity—all on the theory that customers will take more kindly to higher prices than to lousy service.

Mostly because of the higher minimum wage, the fast-food industry's total wage costs are expected to rise about 12% next year, industry analysts say. Wages represent about one-fourth of the restaurant's expenses, so a 12% wage increase means a 3% rise in total costs. And that's about how much prices will go up, analysts predict. Jerrico Inc. recently raised prices in its Long John Silver's restaurants by about 2.5%, indicating the prediction is on target.

Though price rises may average 3% overall, they won't be that amount on all items. McDonald's, for instance, is considering "where we can raise prices without dropping customer acceptance" according to Edward H. Schmitt, president.

Holding the Line

And KFC, beset by flat sales in the last three years, says it won't raise prices at all. The company won't give figures, but it says reducing off-peak work crews has saved more money than the minimum-wage boost will cost—making a price increase unnecessary.

[C]

Instead of just sending some workers home earlier, as KFC is doing, some companies may actually close shop earlier. "With the minimum wage going up, hours that once were marginally profitable might become unprofitable," says John Toby, a vice president of Jerrico, which is considering closing earlier.

Taking another tack, McDonald's has launched a companywide campaign to reduce crew turnover, which now averages three times a year at each restaurant. "Hiring and training costs us money," McDonald's Mr. Schmitt says. "If we can cut down on our turnover, we can reduce a major operating cost."

McDonald's and other companies hope the higher minimum wage will bring in more homemakers, who generally don't come and go as quickly as teen-agers and college students. But "housewives feel out of place working with kids," says Donald Trott, a restaurant analyst with Blyth, Eastman Dillon & Co. "Past minimum-wage increases didn't get them to leave their homes to cook hamburgers or chicken."

Another cost-cutting gambit is a 1974 minimum-wage law provision that allows a restaurant owner to hire up to six students to work up to 20 hours a week at 85% of the minimum wage, provided their work hours don't amount to more than 10% of a company's total.

Because of the six-student limitation, the provision is useless to big employers like the fast-food companies, but it can be attractive to their franchisees. "I hadn't taken advantage of this before, but I plan to now," says Stacy Smith, who owns six Dairy Queen restaurants in Decatur, Ill.

Fast-food chains also will try to offset higher costs by boosting sales. Hardee's recently started a series of discount and two-for-one sales, which it hadn't tried before. Many of the promotions will involve its recently introduced roast-beef sandwich. KFC is switching advertising agencies to try to perk up sales.

Some fast-food chains are turning to machinery to boost productivity. Indianapolis-based Steak n Shake Inc., for example, has installed new automatic cash registers that it expects to save the chain about $840,000 a year by eliminating mistakes—or almost as much as the extra $1 million Steak n Shake expects to pay in higher wages.

Hardee's is getting new cash registers that will be tied into a computer, to track the stores busiest hours and permit more-efficient scheduling.

Bishop Buffets Inc., a chain of 20 cafeterias in the Midwest, is testing overnight slow-cookers to reduce early-morning work to prepare roast beef. The idea is to have some early-shift workers start at 7 a.m. instead of at 6 a.m., cutting their work weeks by five hours. Bishop employes now working 45 hours a week at the minimum wage would get only an extra $2.50 a week—$106 compared with $103.50—after the minimum wage goes up and their hours go down.

The quest for labor-saving machines will continue. "Higher labor costs intensify the search for productivity, and we'll be putting more money into research," says McDonald's Mr. Schmitt. "But I can't tell you that tomorrow we'll be installing machines that cook hamburgers without us having to turn them. It just doesn't work that way."

QUESTIONS AND EXERCISES

(1) Refer to passage A: Without calculating any percentage changes, determine whether the demand by KFC for labor hours is elastic or inelastic. Explain briefly.

(2) Refer to passage B: Using the "least-cost" condition, briefly explain why more automation is being implemented.

(3) Assuming the fast food industry was initially in long-run competitive equilibrium, explain why prices will increase in the short run. Make sure to indicate which of the cost curves will be affected by the increase in labor costs. Explain what will happen in the industry in the long run. Will the long-run price be higher than before the increase in the minimum wage? Explain.

(4) Refer to passage C: State a rule that determines whether a profit-maximizing firm would close earlier as a result of the wage rate increase.

Telephone Pricing of Directory Assistance Calls

CINCINNATI (UPI)—Pam Sanders is one of 370 telephone operators here who do nothing but handle the monthly load of more than 2.25 million "directory assistance" calls.

"Almost all the calls I get are for numbers in the phone book," says Pam, who estimates she talks to 600 callers each three hour work split. "I try to be diplomatic and say, 'the number is listed as . . . ,' but what I really mean is, 'next time look in your book.'

Callers may start looking in the book because soon it's going to cost 20 cents to get the number from Pam or another infor-

mation operator here.

Beginning Sunday, the Cincinnati Bell Telephone Co. will allow its customers only three free information calls a month within the large Southwestern Ohio area code of 513, and then charge 20 cents for all subsequent requests.

And if you dial "O" for the regular operator and request a phone number, it will cost you 40 cents because two operators will be involved.

Cincinnati Bell, which serves about a half-million customers, is believed to be the first

phone company in the nation to charge such a fee. It could be the start of a national trend since other phone companies across the country have filed similar requests with their state utility commissions.

But the move by Cincinnati Bell has not been without opposition.

A citizens protest is being led by Jim Howard Witt, a suburban Fairfield Radio News Director, who believes his "Citizens for Fair Telephone Rates" group is the only stop-gap in what he calls the "telephone domino theory."

EXERCISES

Assume the policy change in the excerpt from the UPI dispatch above can be interpreted as follows: instead of putting the average cost of the directory assistance call into every customer's basic monthly service charge (which means, for all practical purposes, that the price faced by any customer for a directory assistance call is zero), telephone companies want to charge only directory assistance callers for this service at a given price per directory assistance call.

(1) Write one paragraph on the economic efficiency aspects of charging directly for directory assistance calls.

(2) Write another paragraph on the "income distribution" aspects.

Crusader Addresses Women For:
Nader Hits 'Violence' of Big Business

BY MAGGIE SAVOY
Times Women's Editor

Consumer crusader Ralph Nader raised hackles, hair and a standing ovation from 1,000 members of Women For: during a whirlwind, biting talk Monday at the Beverly Hilton.

Intense, with craggy face and dark flashing eyes, this young Harvard graduate who is worse news to corporations and big business than the stock market, raked big business institutions and government.

And he even berated the poor fellows at the bottom of the ladder, who are manipulated, defrauded, overtaxed, cheated, poisoned and powerless, and who are "wasting their time battling red herrings and symbols and each other" instead of trying to right-up an upside-down society.

"We suffer from a gross lack of percepttion," he charged.

"We get all upset by crime on the streets and violence on our campuses. If we'd react with the same vigor to violence from big business, we might do something about it.

Pollution Is Violence

"Our technology is AD 2000.

"And we react to our problems at the 3000 BC level."

Environmental pollution is violence, he pointed out. In terms of cost to our health, safety, and property damage, it "absolutely dwarfs crime in the streets and disorders on the campus in terms of numbers of people affected, seriousness of impact, disastrous effects and property damage."

All the riots this past year did $300 million property damage, he noted. "Our air pollution alone costs us $11 billion a year.

"It is a crime for a man to relieve himself in the Detroit River; but not for an industry to relieve itself in the Detroit River.

"It costs $25 to drop a banana peel in Yosemite. But what fines have been levied for all the havoc to Santa Barbara?

"We talk about the Chicago Seven," he snorts. "Who is prosecuting the Santa Barbara Six?"

An example of upside downness is the worst oil spill ever in the Gulf of Mexico. "Chevon violated 150 regulations; was fined $1.8 millon. That's just a bit more than it takes in gross revenue in one hour. And it pumps 24 hours a day, 365 days a year."

Perception Manipulated

Muggers, he says, are jailed.

"Smoggers aren't . Muggers don't have stockholders."

We have, he says, "allowed our perceptions to be manipulated, our brains to be washed by governmental officials and the men in the corporate suites.

"General Motors grosses $2.4 million an hour, 24 hours a day. Scientists say a $150 million a year research and development budget for any two years in the last 10 would have produced a nonpolluting engine. And yet they spent $250 million just to change all their signs to read, 'GM—Mark of Excellence'.

"We get all upset about militants and radicals; and let U.S. Steel smother Gary, Ind., 24 hours a day."

We do not suffer from lack of technology he points out. "We are at a point now where we can set a goal and reach it. We said we'd get to the moon in 10 years. We made it in nine." Nader, referring to a pamphlet prepared by Women For: took issue with one of its statements: "Consumers in California lose $600 million a year to swindlers. In the Los Angeles marketplace there are more than 52,000 businesses serving 7 million people, and 43 people to police that marketplace. But the city alone hired 164 dog catchers to worry about 300,000 dogs."

"Add a few zeroes," he told his audience. "The nation's fraud bill is $78 billion—including water in hams and turkeys, useless warranties, deceptive packaging."

As for our free enterprise system, it's a myth, he says. "Let a business get in trouble and the president takes the next plane to Washington for subsidies, preferential contracts, tax breaks. What with depreciation and write-offs, our system is better labeled 'Corporate Socialism'—a system which maximizes profits and socializes losses, which the little man makes up in taxes."

Resolutions, pleas, picketing and even boycotts won't help much, Nader warned.

"New politics will not come without new institutions. We need articulate, sustained citizen-action working with professional and technical skills. And recognition that the nature of modern-day political demography is to manipulate groups against each other instead of getting us together on common problems.

"Even at the highest level we do this. We blame our problems on 'yippies, hippies, malcontents and discontents.'

"Our common problems are inflation, war. racism, decaying cities, hunger, consumer abuse, non-responsiveness of agencies.

"I ask you—can any of these problems be blamed on 'yippies, hippies, discontents and malcontents'?"

There is one source of optimism, he believes. "The young, motivated people who are choosing new kinds of career patterns and not going after the buck.

"Turn them off, let them drop out and this country is in serious trouble."

Among those youth are the Nader's Raiders, all of whom worked last summer at "one-half the salary of one affluent corporation attorney in Washington."

This summer Nader had 4,000 applicants among law, economic, science, medical students. "And money for only 175.

"They're a good bargain," he said. "The entire budget for John Schulz's group of six (Schultz is now an assistant professor at USC)was $500. And they shook the Federal Trade Commission to its foundations."

He would like to see such groups formed in every city and county in the country, supported by professionals in the community, advised by lawyers, engineers, economists, and backed by a new kind of involved, informed, committed citizenry.

"Power is not 4 million signatures," he says. "It's marshaling resources. Maybe we can boycott detergents—we got along for generations without them.

"But how can we boycott the automobile? Mass transit has been delayed, voted out or not kept in repair: A person needs a car to get to work or to school.

"Citizens and groups are wasting their time today fighting over highly emotional issues instead of focusing their power, working together against common problems," he added.

"First order is to get rid of our basic ambivalent hypocrisy and reclaim our historical symbols.

"The Flag should stand for peace, justice and equity," he said. "And not for a figleaf covering dishonesties and political cowardice.

"Patriotism shouldn't be the person who agrees with you about the war, but attention paid to what makes up this country—how it runs, who it benefits and what the future direction and qauality of the country will be."

COMMENTS AND QUESTIONS

According to this article, Nader is reported to have said some of the following:

"Environmental pollution is violence; in terms of cost to our health, safety, and property damage it dwarfs crime in the streets and disorders on campus. Riots did damage of $½ billion but air pollution cost $14 billion a year. It is a crime for a man to relieve himself in the Detroit river, but not for industry. It costs $25 to drop a banana peel in Yosemite, but what fines have been levied on all the havoc in Santa Barbara? Muggers are jailed, smoggers are not; muggers don't have stockholders. We have allowed our perceptions to be manipulated, our brains to be washed."

No matter what your views about Nader and his achievements over the past few years, hasn't he omitted something in this indictment? How much pollution should we have?

DAVID B. WILSON

General sales tax merits attention

All over the country, state and city governments are reeling under the one-two punch of simultaneous recession and inflation. Costs are rising, revenues are dropping and the politicians are reaching for the usual remedy — more taxes.

Conservatives long have argued that this is the iatrogenic approach, that is, that the physician is in fact causing the disease. But, as the fiscal crunches come, the politicians and bankers have no choice. They have to get up the cash or public employees and dependents won't get paid, with frightful consequences for society.

When the Federal government forgives a token portion of the personal income tax, the state and local governments and the Social Security system snap the money up and take more. Meanwhile, inflation slices away at people's real wealth.

Less and less of what government at all levels does is adding to that wealth. More and more amounts merely to the debasement of the currency by inflationary public borrowing for purposes of income redistribution.

Our ride on this un-merry-go-round is rendered even less pleasurable by the liberals's preferred method of raising public funds, the steeply graduated, purportedly "progressive" state income tax.

"Soak the rich!" is their rallying cry, even when there aren't that many rich left to soak.

Conservatives who suggest that a fair way of raising money would be a general sales tax on the lines presently in effect in such states as Georgia, California and Michigan are accused of wishing to grind the faces of the poor.

In Massachusetts, it is estimated that a general sales tax of 3 percent levied on the tax base used in Georgia would raise $500 million in addition to the $270 million now raised from sales tax.

Those who argue that such a tax would bear inequitably on the poor tend to forget just what these revenues are used for.

If they were to be used for general government purposes like courts, fire, police, legislatures, defense, water supply or environmental improvement, it might be argued that "ability to pay" should be a prime consideration.

But the money presently being demanded by a government dedicated to income redistribution as a positive moral goal is not for general governmental purposes. It is money being taken from some people to be given to other people.

This Robin Hood ethic is acceptable to the recipients of course. It is even welcome to people who have so much money they can afford to pay either huge taxes or lawyers to help avoid them.

But to people attempting to make their way without benefit of public assistance, the increasing proportion of their earnings being extorted by the tax collector is intolerable. And the withholding system really leaves them no choice.

The proceeds of additional taxation at the state and local level are almost entirely designated for income redistribution. Public assistance, including medical assistance, cut-rate higher education, mass transit systems which do not meet 50 percent of operating costs, housing subsidies, aid to cities inhabited by the almost tax-exempt poor, interest on upward-spiraling debt—all of these are means of transferring wealth from the productive and tax paying sector of society to the un-productive and dependent.

Under these circumstances, the charge of regressiveness simply will not stick to the general sales tax. One might add that middle class taxpayers, ineligible for public entitlements, are often worse off, in terms of disposable income, than people who seem statistically poorer.

A general sales tax is a tax on consumption. It is naturally graduated as people who consume more pay more. The buyer of a $7000 car pays seven times as much as the buyer of a $1000 car. The motorist who makes his old car go another year pays nothing.

In a consumer society, with a general sales tax, the more you buy the more you pay. That amounts to built-in progressiveness. For some reason, the liberals cannot seem to grasp this.

QUESTION

Reasonable people may disagree over the question of whether we should move to a general sales tax. But is progressivity one of its virtues, as this writer suggests?

Courtesy of the Boston Globe. (July 14, 1975).

Part IV

INTERNATIONAL ECONOMIC PRINCIPLES IN ACTION

TRADE EXPANSION ACT OF 1962
STATEMENT OF B. C. DEUSCHLE
IN HEARINGS BEFORE THE
EIGHTY-SEVENTH CONGRESS, SECOND SESSION
COMMITTEE ON WAYS AND MEANS,
HOUSE OF REPRESENTATIVES

Mr. KEOGH (presiding). You are recognized, Mr. Deuschle.

Mr. DEUSCHLE. Thank you, Mr. Chairman.

Mr. Chairman and members of the Committee on Ways and Means, my name is B. C. Deuschle.

I am vice president of the Acme Shear Co., located in Bridgeport, Conn. I appear before this committee as president of the Shears, Scissors & Manicure Implement Manufacturers Association, the only national trade association of domestic manufacturers of scissors and shears.

The scissors and shears industry is a distinct industry and should not be confused with the larger industry and flatware industries.

The association respectfully wishes to record with this committee its strong opposition to H.R. 9900 in its present form. This bill could destroy industries such as our and add to the unemployment problem.

During the past 15 years representatives of our association have appeared before this committee and other congressional committees, the Committee for Reciprocity Information and the Tariff Commission, to present our views on the impact of imported scissors and shears on our domestic industry.

We have never requested or suggested that a complete embargo be placed on the import of scissors and shears. All that we have asked for and desire is a fair competitive opportunity, not an advantage.

To date we have not obtained relief in any form.

We believe that H.R. 9900 would make matters worse. H.R. 9900 provides for new Presidential authority to reduce or eliminate duties. We realize that title III of H.R. 9900 provides for adjustment assistance, but the criteria are general and too much is left to the discretion of the President in granting assistance.

Terms such as "significant," "prolonged," and "reasonable," used in title III to determine if a firm or an industry should receive assistance are subject to many interpretations.

Injury or threat of injury as it is written into our present escape clause cannot be properly defined. When 42 manufacturers out of 50 cease manufacturing and go out of business within 12 years as a direct or indirect result of excessive imports, and the Tariff Commission as well as the President decide that there is no injury or threat of injury, something should be done.

Imports of shears and scissors valued over $1.75 per dozen import value have reached the proportion that they represent 95 percent of domestic production of scissors and shears in this category.

This category represents 75 percent of total sales of all scissors and shears in the domestic market. Would you honestly say, under these circumstances, that there is no injury or threat of injury to our industry?

H.R. 9900 provides for the repeal of section 7 of the Trade Agreements Extension Act of 1951 as amended, the so-called escape clause. The escape clause must not be repealed.

It must be retained and strengthened by amendments to establish definite criteria to guide the Tariff Commission in the determination of injury or threat thereof. And, the Tariff Commission findings of fact in escape clause cases have got to be binding upon the President. If not, we are finished.

The chart on the following page shows better than any words I could use the import problem faced by the domestic scissor and shear industry.

I offer this chart for the record and ask that it be printed immediately following my remarks.

Mr. KEOGH. Without objection, that will be done.

Mr. DEUSCHLE. On the chart is a line which indicates the average level of imports during the prewar years. The sharp increase in imports during 1950 and 1951 were due to a 50 percent reduction in the rate of duty during those years.

Industries such as ours are supposed to be able to obtain relief from injury or threatened injury under the provisions of the so-called escape clause.

The domestic scissor and shear industry has had two escape clause investigations, one in 1953 and again in 1958. Neither of these investigations resulted in any relief for our industry.

Members of the association concluded after the 1958 investigation that it would be futile to request a third investigation until Congress amended the escape clause to restrict the Tariff Commission's interpretative powers and the President's unlimited discretion over the Commission's recommendations.

Now we find ourselves faced with H.R. 9900, which provides for the repeal of the escape clause, the only hope for relief that import ravaged industries have available.

The Secretary of Commerce in his presentation to this committee passed over industries such as ours by stating that they accounted for only a minute part of our gross national product.

We realize that the domestic scissor and shear industry with its 1,000-plus employees accounts for only a fraction of 1 percent of the gross national product, but we see this as no justification for letting the industry be completely destroyed by imports produced with low-cost labor.

[87]

Reprinted from *Hearings Before the Committee on Ways and Means*, 1962, pp. 1656–1659, U. S. Government Printing Office, Washington, D.C.

[A]

The workers in the domestic scissor and shear industry do not want to become wards of the State; they want to use their skills, which have taken years to develop. These workers are not interested in retraining; over many years they have developed a skill they are proud of and want to continue the work they are happy doing.

If the scissors and shears imported during 1961 had been manufactured in the United States, it would have provided over 2 million man-hours of factory work, or full-time employment for over 1,000 American employees.

Domestic manufacturers of scissors and shears have modernized and automated their operations in an effort to meet foreign competition. But foreign manufacturers also have modern equipment and with their lower wage rates are underselling domestic firms in the U.S. market at today's rate of duty.

H.R. 9900 would give the President unrestricted authority to reduce duties and thereby further reduce the cost of imported scissors and shears in our market. Under the provisions of this bill, scissors and shears would be buried in a category with many other items and the duty cut 50 percent.

This would mean a reduction of at least 20 cents per pair at the retail level for scissors and shears now being retailed at $1 to $1.29 per pair.

If this is permitted, we do not need a crystal ball to see the results. There are only eight domestic firms now remaining of the 50 operating in the United States prior to the 50 percent reduction in import duty during 1950–51.

A list of these is attached to my statement which we would very much like to have included in this record.

Mr. KEOGH. Without objection, it will be placed at the conclusion of your testimony.

[B]

Mr. DEUSCHE. These few remaining manufacturers would be forced to close their doors and discharge their employees. The United States would then become wholly dependent on imported scissors and shears.

We cannot understand how it could be in the national interest to permit such a loss. We would lose the skills of the employees and management of the industry as well as the capital investment in production equipment. In the event of a national emergency and imports cutoff, the United States would be without a source of scissors and shears, basic tools for many industries and trades essential to our defense.

The scissor and shear industry is one of the oldest in the world. The skill was brought to the United States from Germany at a time when the United States needed new industry and a scissor and shear industry in particular.

[C]

Scissors and shears of all sizes and types are used in every school, retail establishment, office, factory, hospital, and home in the United States. Scissors cannot be classified as a luxury, gimmick, or novelty.

Scissors are used to separate us from our mothers at birth; to cut our toenails; to trim the leather in our shoes; to cut and trim the materials used in every piece of clothing that we wear.

They are used to cut our fingernails, to trim our mustaches, the hair in our ears and nose, and to cut the hair on our heads—even down to the end of the road when our best suit or dress is cut down the back so that the undertaker can dress us for the last ride. Scissors are truly used from birth to death. They are essential to our health, education, and general welfare.

I ask you gentlemen, is this an industry that should be permitted to become extinct in this country?

We request that the committee not grant the President the authority he has requested in H.R. 9900, but that the bill be amended.

We urge that Congress retain its power over duties as is provided in section 8 of the Constitution.

We request that the escape clause be retained, strengthened, and clearly defined as to what will constitute injury or threat of injury, and we also request that this bill be sent to Congress under open rule procedure.

(Material referred to follows:)

Birmingham Cutlery Co., Birmingham, Ala.
Cameron Manufacturing Co., Emporium, N.Y.
Case-Smiley Co., Fremont, Ohio.
Clayton Manufacturing Co., New York, N.Y.
Crown Cutlery Co., Newark, N.J.
Cueto & Stanek Cutlery Co., Newark, N.J.
Cutlery Corp. of America, Bridgeport, Conn.
Arthur Dorp, Newark, N.J.
Essex Cutlery Co., Newark, N.J.
Harjan, Inc., East Orange, N.J.
A. Henkel Manufacturing Corp., Keene, N.H.
Carl W. Heuser, Irvington, N.J.
International Edge Tool Co., Newark, N.J.
Kafelt Manufacturing Corp., Keene, N.H.
La Cross Manicure Accessories, New York, N.Y.
William Longbein & Bros., Brooklyn, N.Y.
Ernst Melchoir's Cutlery, Irvington, N.J.
Midwest Tool & Cutlery Co., Sturgis, Mich.
Monarch Cutlery Manufacturing Co., North Bergen, N.J.
Carl Monkhaus, Fillicotville, N.Y.
Progress Cutlery Co., Fort Smith, Ark.
Revlon Implement Corp., Irvington, N.J.
Rex Cutlery Corp., Irvington, N.J.
Scheffel Bros., Newark, N.J.
T. E. Schneider, Corp., South Norwalk, Conn.
Smileys, Inc., Fremont, Ohio.
Springfield Cutlery, Springfield, N.J.
Tri-Ess Products, Inc., Jersey City, N.J.
U.S. Shear Co., Bronx, N.Y.
W.L.W. Manufacturing Co., Chicago, Ill.
Wallace Manufacturing Co., West Springfield, Mass.
Wigder Manufacturing Co., Newark, N.J.
Witte & Schmitz Cutlery Co., Bridgeport, Conn.
W. V. Hershey & Sons C., Fremont, Ohio.
Metroloy Corp., Canton, Ohio.

LIST OF EIGHT COMPANIES NOW MANUFACTURING SCISSORS AND SHEARS

Acme Shear Co., Bridgeport, Conn.
John Ahlbin & Sons, Bridgeport, Conn.
Case Shear Corp., Nashville, Ark.
Clauss Cutlery Co., Fremont, Ohio.
W. H. Compton Shear Co., Newark, N.J.
A. Lincoln Co., Bridgeport, Conn.
Wahl Clipper Corp., Sterling, Ill.
J. Wiss & Sons Co., Newark, N.J.

Mr. DEUSCHLE. Mr. Chairman, I would like to thank the chairman and the members of the committee for the time afforded me to present this statement.

Mr. KEOGH. We would like to express our appreciation, Mr. Deuschle, for your being here to give us the views of your industry. Are there any questions?

Mr. KNOX. Thank you, Mr. Chairman.

I should like to compliment you, Mr. Deuschle, in bringing your plight to the committee, which affects the small industry which you are a part of.

In my opinion, it is the small industries of the Nation which have made us as great as we are today. By elimination, of course, we may come into the area of giants instead of the small industry which has

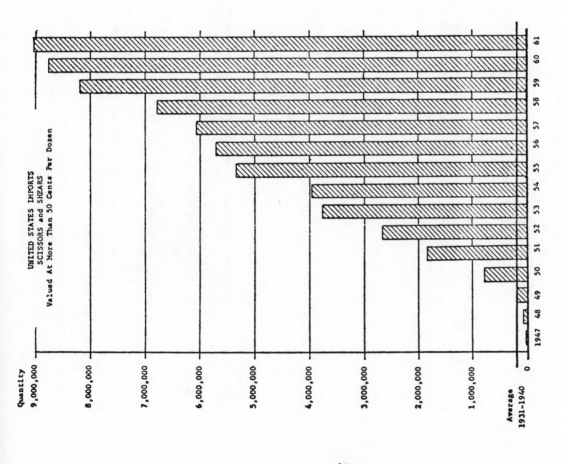

Quantity
9,000,000

UNITED STATES IMPORTS
SCISSORS and SHEARS
Valued At More Than 50 Cents Per Dozen

8,000,000
7,000,000
6,000,000
5,000,000
4,000,000
3,000,000
2,000,000
1,000,000
0

Average
1931-1940

1947 48 49 50 51 52 53 54 55 56 57 58 59 60 61

LIST OF 42 COMPANIES MANUFACTURING SCISSORS AND SHEARS IN 1950 THAT HAVE SINCE CEASED PRODUCTION

Ace Cutlery Co., Newark, N.J.
Atomic Cutlery Co., Irvington, N.J.
H. Balke, Newark, N.J.
H. Boker & Co., Inc., New York, N.Y.
O. J. Bates & Son, Chester, Conn.
Belmar Instrument Co., Belmar, N.J.
Berridge Shear Co., Sturgis, Mich.

Mr. DEUSCHLE, what is the present duty on shears and scissors that are imported?

Mr. DEUSCHLE. The principal category is $1.75 and over, which, as I stated, represents about 75 percent of total domestic scissor and shear consumption. The duty in that category is 10 cents per pair, plus 22.5 percent ad valorem.

This was exactly double that in 1950, before the 50-percent reduction.

Mr. KNOX. May I ask you, then, do you have the percentage rate on the cost? You said about 10 percent.

Mr. DEUSCHLE. Approximately 45 percent.

Mr. KNOX. You would be subject, then, of course, under the provisions of the act, if it were so determined, that the duty could be cut by 50 percent?

Mr. DEUSCHLE. That is correct.

Mr. KNOX. Then, in your opinion, and in many other people's opinion, the industry, itself, would be unable to operate in competition if the duty was cut by 50 percent?

Mr. DEUSCHLE. Yes, sir. You see, in any commodity with a high labor content, foreign competition definitely has the edge.

In Germany, where, incidentally, our own company has a financial interest and we are well aware of what is going on, wages there in our industry are approximately 50 percent or less of ours.

[D]

The labor content in our product is very high. In comparing import dollars with export dollars, the economic imbalance comes in the amount of labor content of the product, not in the dollars.

If we export wheat, which has low labor content, cigarettes, which have low labor content, and we import high labor content products, we create an imbalance that cannot be compared in terms of dollars and cents. [End of D.]

Mr. KNOX. I share your great concern in this problem and assure you that the paper which you have submitted to the committee this morning should be helpful in making our final determinations.

Mr. DEUSCHLE. Thank you very much, sir.

Mr. KEOGH. Mr. Betts, of Ohio.

Mr. BETTS. I was interested in the last page where you list 42 companies that have gone out of business since 1950; is that correct?

Mr. DEUSCHLE. Yes, sir.

Mr. BETTS. Four of those are from Fremont, Ohio. That is close to where I live. Do you or your organization have any figures as to the number of people that were employed at those four plants?

Mr. DEUSCHLE. No, I am afraid we do not. Whatever figures have been made available were made available either by the Commerce Department or by private research organizations who would not divulge knowledge of the individual figures of any company.

The only figures that we have been able to have made available to us are the total figures.

Mr. BETTS. Those four companies went out of business after the reduction, the 50 percent reduction, in tariff; is that correct?

Mr. DEUSCHLE. Yes, sir; they did. That was Case-Smiley Co. of Fremont, Hershey & Metroloy, of Canton, Ohio.

Mr. BETTS. Does your industry enjoy any export business?

Mr. DEUSCHLE. Our export business was quite substantial at one time, but we lost it back in 1950 or 1951. It diminished to practically nothing. I have had some conversations with people in the Commerce Department who claim that there was $1,400,000 worth of cutlery exported from this country, but on investigation we find that the bulk of it is made up of commodities other than scissors and shears.

Mr. BETTS. Mr. Knox asked you about our tariffs on imports. How does it compare with the tariff of other countries on these items?

Mr. DEUSCHLE. I did not quite hear you.

Mr. BETTS. How does our tariff on these products compare with the tariff that other countries have on these products?

Mr. DEUSCHLE. On scissors and shears?

Mr. BETTS. Yes.

Mr. DEUSCHLE. To tell you the truth, I have never checked them because all of the foreign countries could manufacture scissors and shears so much cheaper than we could, and they were all exporting them into this country.

I did not find any need to check their duty restrictions or monetary restrictions or quota restrictions, whatever they might have. There is no need for it. The foreign countries, as I learned on my last trip to France, England, and Italy, feel that they are going to protect their industries, and that is the purpose of the Common Market, to protect their own industries and set up external tariffs to keep damaging competition out of those countries.

It is one of the principal reasons for the Economic Community of Europe. They feel that the time has to come when our wage rates and their wage rates are comparable and that we have a common currency.

[E]

They feel that there will probably be further revaluations of foreign currency, and, of course, they would like to see a devaluation of American currency which, in turn, would help bring us to a more common level.

If this does not happen, it looks as though the administration will force American industry to become competitive on an international basis. There is only one way that it can become competitive on an international basis, and that is if we can reduce our cost to a point where we are competitive.

How do you do that? You have to reduce your cost by automation, mechanization, elimination of labor. This is a wonderful concept, but the large labor unions in this country do not favor this sort of program.

They would like to see wages increased. Unless the administration stops inflation in other quarters, how in the world can they expect American industry to cut costs and automate and get their costs down to a point where they can compete with foreign countries. [End of E.]

...and most of the imports that you mentioned from the Common Market countries?

Mr. DEUSCHLE. The imports in our commodities are largely from Germany, Italy, and Japan. More recently Japan has been climbing and so has Italy. At one time not too long ago Germany was the principal exporter.

They are still leading. Germany is still leading with Italy as the runner-up and Japan follows.

Mr. BETTS. Like Mr. Knox, I was interested in your statement because I think you may have told a story about what might happen to small business if this bill is enacted.

Mr. DEUSCHLE. There is no question about it. I would like to give you one case of a scissors and shears manufacturer in New Jersey that I visited 2 years ago that is no longer in business.

I talked to an old German chap about in his sixties or seventies who came here many years ago because this country needed his skill—his scissor- and shear-making skill.

He came here, he worked hard, he built himself a little factory. He had a sizable mortgage. He raised a family. He built a business manufacturing scissors and shears to the point where he had 50 to 60 employees. The day that I visited him, he had himself, his wife and two sons working. They were working on grinding wheels and his wife was packaging a few pair of scissors. With tears in his eyes he asked me what he was to do.

He said:

I came to this country because they needed me. It was the country of opportunity. After all these years, I am an old man. I trained my boys, I brought them along in this industry, and now we reach the point where this country does not want me anymore. What do you think I can do? Where can I go?

Unfortunately, in that period of 2 years since I last saw him, he died, so we do not have a problem with him anymore.

Mr. BETTS. That is all, Mr. Chairman.

The CHAIRMAN. Are there any further questions?

Mr. KEOGH. Mr. Deuschle, I would like to ask you briefly this question: You indicated in your direct testimony or in response to a question that the wage rate of your industry in Germany is about 50 percent of the wage rate here.

Mr. DEUSCHLE. Approximately.

Mr. KEOGH. My question is: What has been the trend in the wage schedules in Germany over the last 10 years, say? Have they been going up.

[F]

Mr. DEUSCHLE. Up until a year or two ago, there was not too much increase. There was not very much increase in wage rates in Germany, but it has accelerated in the last year or year and a half. However, so have ours. We are in an area, our factories are in areas, I should say, where we are forced to compete with large manufacturers.

If we do not keep raising our wage rates, we do not get any help. We are competing with people like Sikorsky, General Electric, Westinghouse. These are the companies that we have to compete with for labor. So our wage rates and our fringe benefits have increased just as well as theirs, in fact, probably equal. [End of F.]

Mr. KEOGH. The 42 companies that you indicated have gone out of business, have they gone out of business completely or did they convert to making other products?

Mr. DEUSCHLE. Some have gone out completely and others have gone into importing. Some of them are importers. There may be a few that are making other products on a very small scale, but it is negligible.

Mr. KEOGH. Thank you.

The CHAIRMAN. Are there any further questions?

If not, thank you, Mr. Deuschle.

Mr. DEUSCHLE. Thank you, sir.

QUESTIONS

(1) Consider passages B and C: Do they constitute a valid argument for keeping scissor production going in the U.S.?

(2) Consider passage A: If an industry survives because of a tariff, are its workers wards of the state? Would all 1,000 workers be unemployed and worse off forever if the scissor industry ceased to exist?

(3) Consider passage D: Mr. Deuschle thinks he is describing a disaster. In fact he is summarizing a particular explanation of the pattern of trade. Is it a disaster?

(4) Consider passage E: Suppose there was general inflation in America. If the exchange rate were flexible, would this affect any American industry? If it were fixed, would it affect any American industry?

(5) Consider passage F: What does it mean if the scissor industry cannot afford to pay increases granted by other industries?

FORD BARS CURBS ON SHOE IMPORTS; FEARS PRICE RISE

Effects on Consumers Cited —Plan to Assist Industry and Labor Is Backed

By EDWIN L. DALE Jr.
Special to The New York Times

WASHINGTON, April 16— President Ford decided today against imposing higher tariffs or other import restraints on shoes made abroad.

Although the six-member International Trade Commission had found unanimously that the domestic shoe industry was being injured by import competition, today's announcement said the President's decision was "based upon his evaluation of the national interest," including the likelihood of higher prices for consumers if import restraints were imposed.

About 40 percent of all non-rubber footwear sold in the United States is now imported. The main supplying countries are Italy, Spain, Brazil, Taiwan and South Korea.

Most Important Action

In volume of imports, which amounted to $1.1 billion last year, consumer impact and effect on the nation's overall trade policy, the decision today was the most important Presidential trade action in many years.

The domestic industry has been trying for 10 years to obtain relief on the ground that many companies have been forced out of business and thousands of jobs have been lost. It finally won the unanimous injury decision from the International Trade Commission last February under a provision of the 1974 trade law, which has aimed at making it easier for damaged industries to obtain relief.

But the commission could not muster a majority for any particular form of relief. Three members recommended a steep increase in the tariff on imported shoes. Two urged a "tariff quota," meaning a higher duty only on imports beyond a certain volume. The sixth commissioner, Italo H. Ablondi, recommended "adjustment assistance" for companies and workers in the industry, and that is the path the President chose.

Hundreds Certified

It may not mean much in practice. Workers in the industry have already been applying in large numbers for worker assistance, which is chiefly expanded unemployment compensation benefits. The Labor Department has certified hundreds of them as eligible, well before the Presidential decision, and only today 545 more workers from three shoe plants were certified.

As for the companies, there is little experience to indicate how much help adjustment assistance might be. Administered by the Commerce Department, this hitherto small program includes such aid as loans, guaranteed loans and technical assistance. About 300 smaller companies in the industry—the ones who have most suffered from import competition—are considered potential candidates for aid, but it is unclear how many will apply.

The President today instructed the Secretary of Commerce and the Secretary of Labor to ask Congress for additional appropriations if necessary as a result of qualified applications for adjustment assistance in this industry.

Because there was no majority in the commission for any specific form of relief, it appears that Congress cannot override Mr. Ford's decision against imposing import restraints. Where there is a majority finding of injury, and a majority recommendation for relief—as was the case in the recent decision to impose restraints on imports of specialty steel—the President is subject to an overriding vote in Congress if he fails to accept the commission recommendation.

Announcement by Dent

Today's announcement was made not by the President himself nor by the White House but by Frederick B. Dent, the President's Special Representative for Trade Negotiations.

"A remedy involving import restraints would have lessened competition in the shoe industry and resulted in higher shoe prices for American consumers at a time when lowering the rate of inflation is essential," the announcement said.

Mr. Dent made two other major points:

¶"The United States footwear industry is benefiting from a substantial increase in production, shipments and employment as a result of the economic recovery" and "a number of plants have reopened, order backlogs of domestic manufacturers have increased, and profitability has improved."

¶"Import restraints would have exposed United States industrial and agricultural trade to compensatory import conNcessions or [foreign]retaliation against United States exports" under the rules of the general Agreement on Tariffs and Trade.

A "fact sheet" on the decision said the trade commission's own report "casts grave doubt on import relief as an effective remedy" for the smaller companies that have been injured by import competition. Instead, according to the statement, such restraint "would disproportionately benefit the 21 larger firms which produce 50 percent of domestic output but which have been found to be competitive with imports."

'Grave Doubt' Cited

The President was under heavy pressure from both sides in this case. Only last week, George Meany, president of the American Federation of Labor-Congress of Industrual Organizations, urged the President to impose import quotas on shoes, a stronger relief than recommended by any of the trade commissioners.

On the other side, Consumers Union also wrote the President last week urging him "not to impose any tariff, quota or tariff-rate quota, either unilaterally or by negotiations with other countries."

A Cabinet-level body known as the Trade Policy Committee studied the trade commission's decision but was unable to agree on a recommendation to the President. Each member had a chance to argue his case at a meeting with the President in the White House last week.

In the end, according to trade policy officials, the choice came down to several versions of a tariff quota, on the one hand, or adjustment assistance, on the other. The President made it himself, and even high officials did not know what it was until yesterday or today.

Today's decision was taken under the revised "escape clause" provision of the 1974 trade law, which makes possible relief for industries that can show injury from imports. In only one case, the specialty steel one, has relief been provided, though the actual form is for the moment being negotiated with the foreign producing countries.

Nn other major cases are pending before either the President or the International Trade Commission, and no new cases have been filed with the commission since the favorable decision on specialty steel.

(1) Who gains and who loses as a result of Ford's actions on shoe import quotas?

(2) In February 1978, George Meany made a speech at the annual AFL-CIO convention pleading for government intervention to "protect American industry from cut-throat and often illegal foreign competition." What arguments would you offer against tariffs, quotas, or other agreements to restrict imports?

REVIEW & OUTLOOK

The Nickel Peso

We were naturally sorry to see that Mexico, which had held the peso at 12 to the dollar for 22 years, finally threw in the towel on September 1 and let it slide to a nickel. Outgoing President Luis Echeverria Alvarez is being credited with courage in approving the devaluation, bequeathing to his successor the "benefits" of a cheaper peso. But it is hard for us to see the move bringing anything but grief to Jose Lopez Portillo, who becomes president of Mexico on December 1.

[A]

Ironically enough, for the 22 years of the peso's stability it was almost universally believed that a nation's economy could improve through a currency devaluation.

Its export goods become cheaper and more competitive internationally, or so the theory goes. Yet Mexico hung in there manfully, refusing to take advantage of such "beggar-thy-neighbor" policies.

But since 1971, the notion that devaluation spurs production and employment has been so discredited by the record that it's a wonder there are still academics around who are not embarrassed in defending the theory. Yet Mexico has picked this moment to take the plunge, not by a little bit, but by almost 40%. It would be easier to credit Mr. Echeverria with courage if he were beginning his administration with this decision.

The instantaneous effect of the devaluation was to wipe out 40% of the financial assets of peso creditors and 40% of the debt of peso

[B]

debtors. In a strict sense, for every loser there was a gainer, but it's difficult to see how the economy benefits by a one-time government distribution of windfall profits and losses.

Beyond these adjustments in wealth positions, there were the inevitable effects on prices. Californians who rushed down to Tijuana with dollars, figuring on getting 40% off on all traded goods in the Mexican marketplace, discovered that shopkeepers were not accepting pesos, but were insisting on payment in dollars at pre-devaluation levels. And further from the border, where dollars are not as widely in circulation, prices in pesos were being marked up by the full amount of the devaluation.

[C]

The only way the devaluation can possibly work in theory is if prices rise by less than the amount of the devaluation. So the government, which controls prices, had to crack down on businessmen and shopkeepers who were putting prices up for mere survival. As has been true throughout history, though, when people are forced to sell their goods or labor at prices lower than the market values them, they will either refuse to produce or create a black market.

Mr. Echeverria seems determined to follow through on his courageous, destructive course. But come December 1, Mr. Portillo will have an opportunity to at least take those measures that can keep Mexico from sliding further into

[D]

recession and inflation. First, he has to persuade potential creditors that this devaluation was it, and that the nickel peso will be good for at least another 22 years. Secondly, he must permit prices to rise or Mexico will become one big black market. Finally, because the entire work force will be shifted well upward into higher personal income-tax brackets because of the devaluation's effects on prices and wages, there must be downward tax-rate adjustments and soon, or the resultant disincentive effects will send unemployment climbing even faster than it has.

"The devaluation has at least provided an excuse for tax reform, but it must come quickly," says Robert Mundell of Columbia University. Professor Mundell, an international economist, also believes Mexico could extract benefits from the process if, in addition, it reverts to its practice of the past 22 years of automatically pegging to the dollar. Foreign creditors, those who lost most heavily, have to believe it won't happen again. "The devaluation was big enough so it can't be argued it wasn't sufficient, and that's all to the good," he says.

The nickel peso could and should have been avoided, if Mexico had only kept its monetary policy tied to the U.S. Federal Reserve's as it had for 22 years. But what's done is done, and the incoming president will somehow have to make the best of it. More than courage, he'll need correct economic advice instead of obsolete theory.

(1) Is it *always* true that a nation's economy will improve through a currency devaluation?

(2) What other effects is the peso devaluation likely to have besides income distribution?

(3) Why might price controls interfere with the desirable effects of the peso's devaluation?

(4) Will it be in the interest of Mexico to guarantee a nickel peso for the next 22 years? Are there any good economic reasons for pegging the peso to the dollar?

Strain on 'Snake' Eases as Central Banks Move to Prop Danish, Belgian Currencies

A WALL STREET JOURNAL *News Roundup*

Pressure eased yesterday on the joint European currency float as central banks intervened to lift two of the "snake" participants off the floor.

But analysts viewed the development as merely a temporary respite from the economic forces that are pushing to realign the European currnecy bloc.

Dealers noted that overall dealings yesterday were light. The U.S. dollar was narrowly mixed.

[A]

The Danish and Belgian central banks were the main factors in yesterday's trading. They intervened to push up the Danish krone and the Belgian franc, which both had been nestling on the snake floor, against the West German mark, the long-term strong man of the joint float. The Belgian franc closed the second highest currency in the bloc, after the mark. It was followed by the Danish krone, Swedish krona, Norwegian krone and Dutch guilder.

Removes Strain on Snake

The action removed the strain on the snake, which limits the participating currencies to a band 2¼% above and 2¼% below their declared parity rates against each other. They float as a bloc against the dollar and other funds.

[B]

Few dealers viewed yesterday's currency movements as a lasting solution to the snake's basic problem. They believe the mark is undervalued against such weaker currencies as the Danish krone and Belgian franc.

"The swing has been tremendous, fantastic, and the stresses and strains have been entirely eliminated—for the moment," a London leader said. "But we just might see it all swing back. It's out of line. The Belgian franc's at the bottom one day and near the top the next, and that doesn't reflect economic reality. Why should it suddenly be stronger than the Dutch guilder?"

May Take Pressure Off

The widely held belief is that basic economics will force a formal realignment of the snake's assigned parities.

But short-term market forces may take the pressure off, for a bit. Speculators may find, for instance, that they can't maintain for long the positions they took in gambling on a quick realignment. Unwinding these positions could tend to reverse the basic pressures, strengthening the weak sisters at the expense of the stronger ones.

The dollar yesterday had an uneven day. In Frankfurt, it rose to 2.5395 German marks from 2.5343 on Friday. It eased in Zurich to 2.5375 Swiss francs from 2.5360. In London, the pound inched up against the dollar to $1.9212 from $1.9210.

French dealers saw yesterday's market as a "breathing spell." The feeling that "something is going to happen" seemed a consensus. In Paris, the dollar fell to 4.7113 French francs from 4.7225.

Italian Economy

Banca di Roma, a large commercial bank 89.2%-owned by the Italian government, said in a monthly newsletter that Italy's economy seems to be recovering slightly but that uncertainty continues to cloud the scene. Against that backdrop, the dollar dropped in Milan to 847.50 lire from 857.50.

[C]

Some analysts said austerity measures announced by the Rome government last week were a possible factor in the lira's comeback. But one Milan dealer said the Italian fund gained mostly "because the big purchasers of dollars last week, such as oil importers, kept away from the market."

On the Tokyo foreign-exchange market, the dollar recovered a bit Monday, rising to 299.93 yen from 299.78.

The U.S. currency eased, though, in Montreal, with the Canadian dollar gaining to $1.0153 (U.S.) from $1.0148.

Another very quiet day on bullion markets saw gold's price edge up 15 cents an ounce. The five major London dealers raised their common quote 40 cents an ounce at their morning meeting, but they cut it back 25 cents in the afternoon, to $133.75 an ounce.

QUESTIONS AND EXERCISES

(1) Regarding passage A: Illustrate the effect of the Central Bank action in Denmark and Belgium on a supply-demand diagram for foreign exchange (one for each country).

(2) Regarding passage B: What does it mean to say the "mark is undervalued against such weaker currencies as the Danish krone and the Belgian franc"?

(3) Explain passage C with the aid of supply-demand diagrams.

INDEX OF KEY CONCEPTS

*This index contains an alphabetical listing of the key concepts cited in the front matter. Page numbers refer to the first page of an article in which a concept can be found.